Peter S. Fisher
Siegfried the Wrestler

Lettre

Peter S. Fisher received a Ph.D. in Modern European History from Harvard University. His research interests are history and popular culture of the Kaiserreich and Weimar Republic.

Peter S. Fisher

Siegfried the Wrestler

The Wilhelmine World of a Colportage Novel

[transcript]

Bibliographic information published by the Deutsche Nationalbibliothek
The Deutsche Nationalbibliothek lists this publication in the Deutsche Nationalbibliografie; detailed bibliographic data are available in the Internet at http://dnb.d-nb.de

Cover layout: Jan Gerbach, Bielefeld
Cover illustration: Anonymous Illustrator. Siegfried and Kanzurow are ready to wrestle in front of the Tsar and Tsarina. Pamphlet Nr. 80 from "Das Weib des Ringkämpfers" (Dresden: Dresdner Roman-Verlag, 1907).

https://doi.org/10.14361/9783839466919
Print-ISBN 978-3-8376-6691-5
PDF-ISBN 978-3-8394-6691-9
ISSN of series: 2703-013X
eISSN of series: 2703-0148

Contents

Part One

Part Two

Part One

1. Three Readers: George Grosz, Moritz Bromme, Adelheid Popp

Readers of colportage literature were unlikely to leave written accounts of their reading habits. There were two reasons for this. First, the multiple stigmas attached to being labeled a colportage or Schund [trashy literature] reader would inspire few people to admit to occupying themselves in this lowly sphere. Lack of education or literary taste were seen as hallmarks of such readers. So too were poverty or youthfulness. Second, a class divide separated readers from non-readers. Lower class members tended to write few autobiographies where reading preferences might be discussed. This leaves us today with a large amount of material written by Schundkämpfer [fighters against trashy literature], the mainly middle class opponents of popular literature, and very little written by people who consumed and enjoyed the "backstair novels" [Hintertreppenromane] distributed by an army of door-to-door salesmen or colporteurs.

George Grosz (1893–1959), the expressionist-modernist artist, was one of the few fans of colportage who remained unembarrassed when he recollected his youthful fascination. Growing up in the Pommeranian town of Stolp, Grosz felt drawn to a literary genre that excited his imagination and made him realize how wide the world was and how full of drama. His main source of colportage was a cluttered, ramshackle stationery store that included a lending library. Such school supply stores that earned additional income by loaning and selling pamphlet literature to their young customers caught the hostile attention of the very vocal Schundkämpfer. In the decade prior to the war, conflicts increased between them and owners of stationery stores.

We do not know if the store frequented by young Grosz was caught in this crossfire. His detailed description of the place evoked its magnetic attraction. A quirky, elderly woman owned the shop whose pens, pencils, erasers, cutting and modeling sheets, and other school materials were stacked into cardboard containers. The backroom was stuffed with old books and tied-up packs of serial novels. Clutching her cane, the bespectacled lady held sway over her kingdom, drawing children to her like "the living witch in the Grimm fairytales."[1]

> It was disorderly. Dust everywhere. The old gas lamp hummed... enveloping the store's interior in semi-darkness like in a Rembrandt painting. The cozy feeling elicited some of us occasionally to abscond with some minor wares. A paper jumping jack hung on the door, a white cardboard skeleton hung next to a hunchbacked Bajazzo clown. Grotesque masks lay up top in a torn box. A false beard lay next to packs of colored chalk, sponges, and small chalkboards. It was a sort of magical garbage dump. Past years' Christmas decorations still adorned the display window. Then there was a dark bluish-black cat who appeared everywhere, it was rumored he could climb along the ceiling like a fly. There were also fine, long crocheted silver threads for Christmas trees – or were they ancient spider webs? Yes, and then everywhere the Hintertreppenromane. Servant girls who had finished reading them, sold and left the grease-stained pamphlets here for a few pennies.[2]

The fantastic titles of this literature remained so impressed on young Grosz's mind that he could recall them in his autobiography fifty years later: Hass und Liebe oder zwei Frauen unter einem Dache (Hate and Love or Two Women under a Single Roof, 1902), Räuberhauptmann Zimmermann, der Freund der Armen, der Schrecken der Tyrannen (Highwayman Captain Zimmermann, Friend of the Poor, Horror of Tyrants, 1904–1905), Dornröschen oder die Verfolgung um die Erde (Sleeping Beauty or Pursued Around the Globe), Fünfundzwanzig Jahre Lebendig Begraben oder Dolch, Kreuz und Liebe (Buried Alive for

Twenty-five Years or Dagger, Cross, and Love), Die Wilddiebe oder die Räuberbraut vom Bayrischen Wald (The Poachers or the Brigand Bride from the Bavarian Forest).[3] "Such beautiful titles," reminisced Grosz, showing none of the retrospective disdain others would display in their memoirs when they recollected youthful reading habits. "I read all the pamphlets that I could purchase," Grosz recalled, noting also that he and his friends traded and borrowed from each other. "The plots were always pretty much the same but this inadequacy did not bother me."[4]

His honest commentary reveals the compelling nature of the material – not unlike many forms of popular entertainment that would be spawned after the age of the installment novel had passed (the very last German installment novels were printed in the 1950s). That anyone could read this "miserable stuff" with pleasure perplexed and angered a generation of Schundkämpfer, but Grosz scorned these so-called educated readers for their inability to give up momentarily their high culture prejudices in order to enjoy a whimsical thriller. He saw them as "stuffed shirts" whom he loved to ridicule in his satirical art, often hinting at and illustrating their own scurrilous fantasies and obscene desires. "The more coarse and improbable the plot, the more engrossed I became over the daring feats, with their fairytale dimensions...," he admitted.[5]

One of the few German intellectuals who had sympathy for such youthful reading habits was Siegfried Kracauer. Writing in the 1920s when the battle over trashy literature reached its zenith, he used the term Knabenlogik [boyhood logic] to describe an alternative approach or mode of reading that educated adult critics needed to consider if they wanted to understand the attractions of this excoriated literature.[6] Youths and many, mostly undereducated adult readers loved these incredible stories and liked identifying with their invincible heroes. Grosz described how in one novel two young heroes managed to outfox a diabolical mechanism that used metal skeletons to embrace and kill intruders to a freemason's lodge. "In my imagination, I saw myself with a friend of mine overcoming this adventurous challenge," he remembered, adding that "the mild chill tickled my fancy."[7] Somehow these stories managed to tantalize, to stimulate, and even to bolster self-confidence.

While Grosz recorded his reading of colportage as experiences of delight and reward, a more typical, disapproving recollection was that of factory worker Moritz Bromme (1873–1926). He criticized serial novels as nothing more than cheap, escapist distraction and an enormous waste of time. Bromme originally wanted to become a teacher but the modest means of his family would not allow it. He became a factory worker and spent time successively manufacturing buttons, wooden clogs, and machines. He joined the Social Democratic Party and eventually became editor of a SPD newspaper. In his 1905 autobiography, Lebensgeschichte eines modernen Fabrikarbeiters (Life Story of a Modern Factory Worker), he described at length his encounters with colportage, both as a reader and as a seller.

At one point in his arduous employment as a worker, he decided to switch to the job of colporteur: "Here at least I was in the fresh air."[8] The seventeen-year-old salesman must have been a persuasive vendor for he recalled signing on fifty subscribers for Karl May's Der verlorene Sohn oder der Fürst des Elends (The Lost Son or the Prince of Misery, 1884–1886). Besides "classic" highwaymen novels like Schinderhannes and Rinaldo Rinaldini, he also hawked Die Waldmühle an der Tschernaja (The Forest Mill on the Tschernaja River, 1881–1882), Amanda die Verstossene oder des Vaters Fluch – der Mutter Segen (Rejected Amanda, Father's Curse, Mother's Blessing, 1890), and Die geheimnisvolle Maske oder im Zauber der Liebe (The Mysterious Mask or the Magic of Love, 1890).[9] Despite his talents, this job did not last long. The youth was noticed, by an acquaintance of his boss, taking an unapproved break at a swimming pool. The employer came to the pool and gave Bromme a public beating with his umbrella. Afterwards, Bromme returned his satchel of promotional materials to the boss's wife. When she asked why he was giving the pamphlets back, he angrily replied that her husband could carry out the samples himself.

While his career as a colporteur was brief, he continued to consume the popular literature in a thrifty manner typical of the working class. Bromme remembered how the oral reading of an episode from an installment novel was often the focal point of an evening's entertainment for family, friends, and in-house tenants. To save money, one person would subscribe to the novel so that a whole group could enjoy it. Using Bromme as an example, we can see the relative costs of such cheap fun. At the button factory, Bromme was paid eight to nine marks a week.[10] One installment (usually issued weekly) cost ten pfennig and the complete one hundred parts totaled ten marks, or more than a week's salary.

> In the evening hours usually Paul Beuer read aloud from a trashy novel. First we got Rinaldini. Next came Waldmühle an der Tschernaja. After a while, I got tired of the horrible deeds of Prince Kasansky who mercilessly beat his serfs and I also tired of the endless battles with the local wolves. I couldn't stop these readings, however, because our tenants and my parents were crazy about them. At one point, they even managed to persuade me to read aloud. The longer I stayed in the factory where my contact was uniformly with uneducated colleagues, the more I forgot my good school education. Instead of building on education, I succumbed to trashy literature. My debut as an evening reader was Die schwarze Maske (The Black Mask). Then it was the turn of Die Todtenfelder von Sibirien oder das Geheimnis des russischen Kaiserschlosses (The Death Fields of Siberia or the Secret of the Russian Imperial Palace, 1890–1891): "A real horror story in which the Romanovs naturally do not look good. The heroes are Michael Bakunin and the fictitious German nobleman Hugo von Pahlen. The latter joins the nihilists because a Russian archduke raped his sister. And so it went until finally, one day, I came upon the speeches and writings of Lassalle (Ferdinand Lassalle, 1825–1864, was one of the founders of the SPD). I didn't just read them, I devoured them. With one stroke, I discovered the right path for my reading. Everything else fell away.[11]

This sort of conversion experience accompanying the discovery of socialist literature and the abrupt turning away from colportage "trash" also characterized the memories of a working class woman. At age ten Adelheid Popp (1869–1939) was already working long hours at crocheting and sewing. In her teens, she worked as a house servant and then moved on to factory employment. Twelve hours of work was the norm. With her tiny savings she rented books, principally colportage: "In addition to highwaymen novels that captured my attention, I had a lively interest in the fate of unfortunate queens."[12] Favorites were Die weisse Frau in der Hofburg zu Wien (The Female Ghost in the Hofburg Palace of Vienna, 1870) and Kaiserssohn und Baderstochter (The Emperor's Son and the Barber's Daughter, 1870). Popp felt that these stories provided her with an escape from reality and transported her into different, exotically interesting historical periods. She liked reading "the novels of one hundred pamphlets" where "a poor girl overcame many scary obstacles before she turned into a countess or at least the wife of a businessman or factory owner. I lived in a sort of delirium. I consumed one installment after another; I was carried away from reality and identified myself with my books' heroines. In my mind I repeated what they said. I felt their fear when they were walled in, buried alive, poisoned, stabbed or tortured. Consciously, I was in a completely different world and saw nothing of the misery surrounding me, nor did I feel my own misery."[13]

Like Moritz Bromme, she became an oral reader for family and friends. She recalled that at age fifteen, during the factory lunch break, the other girls laughed at her when they saw her engrossed in Der Raubritter und sein Kind oder Die Morgenröthe einer neuen Zeit (The Brigand and his Child or the Dawn of a New Era, 1880–1881). For Popp, as well as for the Viennese servant girls studied by Martina Tichy in Alltag und Traum (1984), colportage novels became a form of vicarious living, substituting exciting adventure for the boring drudgery of real life.[14] This alternative reality, Tichy notes, "offers the extraordinary... extreme feelings, the really great passions."[15] Colportage provided, at least in the imagination, "the sparkling life from which servants are excluded."[16]

Picture 1: The illustrated cover and title of this pamphlet points to the primary audience for the novel: <u>The Romantic Dream of the Count's Bride: The Loving and Suffering of a Factory Girl</u>. Written by Ernst Falkenberg [pseudonym]. Published by Adolf Ander, 1909.

Along with the function of overcoming emotional drought and evoking stimuli in an otherwise flat and monotonous reality, Popp found her reading material initiated her interest in history and politics. Lacking a formal education, she took her history lessons from whatever sources she was exposed to. Her mother knew an old man who enjoyed explaining history to the eager listener. A favorite topic was Emperor Maximilian's misadventure in Mexico, a dramatic subject that served as a plot for eight installment novels: "Back then I raved about emperors and queens, and high class people played an important part in my imagination. I had a lively interest in everything political."[17]

Popp began reading a conservative Catholic newspaper that attacked social democracy. She came across antisemitic pamphlets that convinced her Jews were engaging in ritual murder.[18] Popp sought to persuade her fellow workers to boycott Jewish stores. This rather haphazard, confused passage from colportage to rudimentary political thoughts and actions evidences a tangled connection between popular literature and politics. Imaginary excitement evolved into real world agitation. Emotionalized colportage fantasies were rendered and replaced, in one case, by the melodrama of ritual murder and the resulting outrage.

Adelheid Popp, however, did not get stuck in the antisemitic rut. Exposed to social democratic newspapers, she began to see things from a new perspective. Colportage's "brooding sentimentality" and the "destiny of some queen" no longer interested her. The colportage melodrama with its conservative, patriarchal frame of mind gave way to a more sober, egalitarian socialist one. Now, during factory lunch breaks, she read SPD newspaper articles aloud to her co-workers and explained class repression and exploitation. Through their story lines, the installment novels preached acceptance of one's fate and making the most of what destiny had assigned. Social democracy, in contrast, asked for collective action and change. Socialist literature brought into focus the real problems faced by workers, while colportage gave its obfuscated, rose-colored view of the world.

Can we thus generalize from Bromme's and Popp's experiences that colportage literature distracted the reader from reality by offering a mushy, sentimental philosophy calling on the individual to bear one's cross with humility and forbearance? From the colportage perspective, the new, revolutionary views would self-destruct in the face of transcendent forces that truly moved the universe. The populist conservative doctrine espoused by colportage was a part of "the melodramatic mode" developed in France and England in the early nineteenth century. It was not a clearly elaborated, cohesive system of thought. Yet it consistently shines through more than a century of popular literature and theater. Were its innumerable readers unable to see its deleterious effects, its tendency to inject an ideology of political incapacitation? Critics of mass culture in general view its chief defect to be the stifling of a critical consciousness and a diversion away from considering reforms and structural improvements to society. While this view certainly has its valid points, in the case of colportage, it neglects two significant aspects of reader experience. First are the elements esteemed by the readers themselves as positive, even liberating. Second, one needs to consider the reasons for the unrelenting hostility against colportage manifested by Germany's ruling class, the ostensible beneficiaries of a popular ideology that preached "don't rock the boat." If installment novels had the effect of supporting and keeping the system intact (as critics of mass culture maintained), why was the system bent on destroying them?

2. For and Against Popular Literature

Janice Radway's seminal study, Reading the Romance: Women, Patriarchy, and Popular Literature (1984), provides insights to the reading of colportage despite the fact that the readers she examined were living in another country almost a century later. "Reading to escape the present is neither a new behavior nor one peculiar to women who read romances," she noted. The term "escape" carries pejorative connotations, implying that the reading is an activity that simply wastes time and has no intrinsic value. On the contrary, Radway discovered from her interviews that for her readers the act of reading itself was seen as significant. For them, it meant a well-deserved break from the endless labor of being a housewife always dedicated to the well-being of others. While they spent many hours attending to monotonous household chores, the daily reading of a romance fiction gave these women a modest sense of control and a feeling of considerable pleasure. Scholars of popular culture tend to disparage such pleasure as vicarious, ephemeral, and useless. Radway, however, discusses the psychological views that see in this sort of pastime a therapeutic value and she concludes (for her romance readers) that "although this experience is vicarious, the pleasure it induces is nonetheless real."[1] This seemingly simple but important insight helps explain why the reading of "light" popular literature has had enormous appeal across time periods and cultures. Radway asks that the need for "escape" must be reconsidered in modern societies where "individual labor is often routinized, regimented, and minimally challenging."[2] Agreeing that the reading of romances does not spark political action or a call for change, Radway observes: "the romance's short-lived therapeutic value, which is made possible and necessary by a culture that creates needs it cannot fulfill, is finally the cause of its repetitive consumption."[3]

Radway's insights can be applied to the popular reading milieu of Wilhelmine Germany where conditions for low-paid or domestic labor were considerably worse than the conditions experienced by American romance readers of the 1980s. Radway's impressions may also help explain why the reading of colportage, a century earlier, was increasingly viewed with hostility by educators, churchmen, and government officials. Children might decide to read colportage instead of doing homework or listening to teachers or parents; servants could read it instead of completing domestic tasks; housewives could enjoy indulging a pamphlet story break instead of cooking, cleaning, sewing, or tending to children; factory workers may have taken their minds off of boring, mechanized work and drifted into exciting colportage-inspired fantasies. Official Germany monitored the phenomenon of colportage with suspicion and alarm. It warned readers of the multiple menaces they faced. The well-organized opponents of trashy literature even maintained that this reading led directly to a life of crime or even degeneration into insanity.

The battle against colportage was part of a larger war against mass culture and the abundant new forms of entertainment produced in the decades before World War I. Lynn Abrams described the middle class's campaigns against tavern dance halls and the popular variety shows known as Tingel-Tangel.[4] Public funds were invested in planning parks and libraries to counter what the authorities saw as a rise in problematical amusements and widespread hedonism. Public parks were meant to provide urban residents a place for wholesome leisure activity like taking a walk with the family. Public libraries could provide first and second generation readers with good, uplifting literature as an alternative to trashy installment novels.[5] After studying multiple aspects of Wilhelmine working class culture, Abrams asked: "Would workers, whose taste for reading had been stimulated by pamphlet fiction and serialized stories, transfer their allegiance to the more serious and demanding material held in public libraries. The short answer is no."[6] German classics or SPD literature were not going to entice many readers who wanted excitement and sensation, not "uplifting art" or political agitation.

Cinema, at first regarded "as little more than trashy literature in moving pictures," and sports also appealed to growing numbers of workers.[7] Soccer clubs sprang up in cities where spectators could number in the hundreds or thousands. Boxing and wrestling matches occupied a hazy zone between sideshow acts, (like those of muscle men at popular fairs) and sports with standardized rules. Wherever large amounts of people gathered, order needed to prevail and efforts were made to reduce coarse, rambunctious behavior that could easily get out of hand. Cock fighting and bear baiting were condemned by cruelty to animal associations [Tierschutzvereine]. Alcohol was a persistent problem. The many taverns frequented primarily by male workers and artisans posed a challenge for the police.

A form of popular entertainment that drew middle class spectators as well as the working class was the traveling circus. In some of the larger cities, permanent circuses were established and based in large buildings instead of tents. All in all, commercial mass culture grew and satisfied the needs of people in Wilhelmine society: "Women entered the recreation scene in large numbers for the first time. Young people became probably the most voracious consumers of all kinds of entertainment."[8] At the beginning of World War I, special laws gave the authorities a welcome excuse to shut down practically every form of amusement. Dancing was prohibited for the duration of hostilities. The long-contested existence of popular literature now became the prerogative of regional military commands. Trashy literature became a victim as the army could cancel peacetime press laws. Succumbing to Schundkampf pressure groups, military commands issued long lists of books to be pulped. Among them was Das Weib des Ringkämpfers oder Manneskraft und Frauenherz (The Wrestler's Wife or Manly Strength and Womanly Heart, 1907), which had been displayed, with many other serial novels, at the 1911 Reichstag exhibition against trashy literature.

Picture 2: Russia was a favorite backdrop for colportage's melodramatic plots. The violent nihilists provided the kind of spice and excitement the potboiler writers were looking for. American import Nick Carter was the most popular of the new self-contained serial stories. Note how the American cover with title in English was simply incorporated in the German issue. (Nick Carter Band 64, "In der Gewalt der Terroristen," Dresden: A. Eichler, c.1908).

Sponsored by the German Center for Youth Welfare and the German Writers Memorial Foundation, the exhibition drew considerable interest. Friedrich Rommel included his impressions in an article "A Dangerous Enemy of Our Youth" and wished to persuade people to make time for a visit. The displays were arranged in large rooms on the third floor of the Reichstag. On the railings of the staircase leading up to the exhibition, exhibitors fastened Nick Carter pamphlets with their "frightening" and "creepy" covers.[9] These were part of what Rommel described as "a mud slide" of trashy literature flowing across the Atlantic from America. The first exhibition room showed pamphlets that Rommel felt had a special quality of authenticity because they had been "collected" directly from welfare asylums, schools, machine and craft shops, hospitals, and dormitories for homeless people. Here, Rommel identified what he labeled as "old acquaintances." These were dime novels like Luftpiraten (actually Der Luftpirat, ca.1908-1911), Störtebecker (actually Klaus Störtebecker, 1908–1909), Ethel King (1910–1915), and Nat Pinkerton (c.1910-1915). What excited him most and inadvertently revealed an undisguised morbid interest on his part were the Wanda von Brannburg pamphlets that he had not previously seen. Wanda was heralded as a "German master detective" capable of "amazing deeds bordering on the unbelievable." One of the most popular episodes was the case of the sausage factory whose meat, Wanda discovers, was actually the flesh of murdered girls. "Surely the reader thinks 'disgusting' [Pfui Teufel]," observed Rommel and added, "I heard this expression of deep revulsion many times at the exhibition."[10]

Leaving behind the self-contained dime novel stories, the next room was dedicated to the older form of popular literature, the serial novels. Rommel picked out several sensational titles to give prospective visitors a sense of what they could certainly not want to miss: Gertrud das Opfer des Mädchenschlächters (Gertrud the Victim of the Butcher of Girls). Paradoxically, the crusader against trashy literature either consciously or unconsciously changed the title slightly, thereby increasing its luridness. The actual title was Gertrud das Opfer des Mädchenhändlers (Gertrud the Victim of the White Slavery Trader, 1904). Then he noted Schön Lieschen, die lebendig Eingemauerte (Pretty Lieschen, Walled Up

Alive), actually Schön Lieschen der Lindenwirtin Töchterlein oder die lebendig Eingemauerte des Nonnenstein (Pretty Lieschen the Linden Innkeeper's Daughter or Walled Up in the Nonnenstein, 1897).[11] Precision was not a virtue of this Schundkämpfer, nor was the honest exploration of the matter at hand. As with other crusaders, the opponents of trashy literature revealed more about their own social anxieties than they did about problems intrinsic to the objects of their hatred.

"It warmed my heart and I could only smile sympathetically," Rommel noted in a sweet and sour observation, "when I read a proposition made in a Berlin newspaper that we could best oppose trashy literature by simply ignoring it."[12] The innocent layman's naivete called for a rebuke from the expert: "No! No again! German teachers stop brooding in your parlors and engage in the battle against trashy literature which threatens to poison our national soul [Volksseele]."[13] Das Weib des Ringkämpfers oder Manneskraft und Frauenherz was another title that grabbed his attention and was the only compound title that he managed to transcribe accurately. The illustrated cover of Das Zigeunerkind (The Gypsy Child, 1902–1903) aroused his ire because "the publisher used a peculiar trick to satisfy the sensational needs of the reading rabble [Lesepöbel]." Underneath the "sickeningly sweet" picture of the heroine, a question was addressed to the potential reader, "Who is the mother of this child?"[14] Rommel angrily argued that the authors were thus insinuating that the novel was based on actual facts. By making this point Rommel revealed how little he knew about this literature as the claim to verisimilitude was a stock feature of colportage. The contemptuous reference to the readers as rabble showed the crusader's frustrations with the ongoing problem, but also a combination of disdain for the supposedly lower class readers and a certain fear of them. More sympathetic to the working class reader was a socialist writer who was neither pleased nor surprised by the worker's predilection for trashy literature: "He does not expect intellectual stimulation or a lifting of his aesthetic judgment. He only wants to be released from the ongoing desolation of his overworked days, his boring environment. Thus, he welcomes the strongest stimulants."[15]

Picture 3: The cover illustrates the <u>Schundkämpfer's</u> self-image as a knight in shining armor defending Germany from the menace of trashy literature. He stabs at best-selling Nick Carter pamphlets and then consigns them to the flames. (Cover of <u>Festschrift der deutschen Dichter-Gedächtnis Stiftung zum 10 jährigen Bestehen, 1901–1911</u> , Hamburg, 1912).

One visitor to the Reichstag exhibition, Lilli Janosch, complained that it conveyed the impression that the craving for sensation and lasciviousness was virulent only among the lower classes.[16] In addition to cheap trashy literature, she objected, one ought to have included examples of expensive trashy literature, the kind that the middle and upper classes liked to read. Erotic and sexually explicit books were usually too expensive for the lower classes, but affordable for the bourgeoisie and not subject to censorship if held to be of "artistic merit." Janosch ascertained that Berlin theaters, cabarets, and variety halls were also too expensive for workers and their programs illustrated all sorts of themes taken directly from trashy literature. The organizer of the Berlin exhibition, Ernst Schultze, mentioned the fact that, on trains, middle class travelers would read Nick Carter, taking care to remove the pamphlet covers so that no one could see what kind of material they were reading.[17]

Schultze was recognized as one of Germany's leading experts on trashy literature. He was pleased to see that the problem was gaining more serious attention as it "spread from dark corners of society into the public at large."[18] American imports like Nick Carter, Buffalo Bill, and Nat Pinkerton were now the focal point of interest, but Schultze warned that the old potboiler serial novels continued to pose a real threat to youth and uneducated adults. Publishers trained Grub Street writers to manipulate their easy prey: "The scribblers are told to heighten the readers suspense to the point of madness at each episode's end so that he obliviously purchases the next installment."[19] The cliffhanger technique and the order to give the reader ongoing waves of goose bumps was illustrated in the starkest possible manner in the recently published Der Unbekannte. Sensationelle Enthüllungen eines Mädchenmörders (The Unknown Man. Sensational Revelations of a Girl Murderer, 1910). Schultze could find nothing redeeming in the reading of such egregious trash. He dismissed the view that reading colportage at home among the family could be a positive counterweight to far worse alternative forms of amusement like getting drunk at a pub. Schultze also wanted to make sure that no one would be misled by colportage publishers' nefarious efforts to pass off their lucrative novels as patriotic or Christian fare. Injecting national or religious themes was simply a form of camouflage intending to make the material seem rather harmless to readers as well as concerned government officials. Here the crusader felt called upon to share his own face-to-face experiences with the deceitful, abhorrent literature: "Whoever has read a Schundroman or at least a few installments – an educated person can hardly stomach plowing through 1,200 to 2,400 pages – will know how repugnant it is that this cant, this misuse of great and time-honored things should all be done solely in the interest of filthy business. The manner in which these moralizing parts are unexpectedly filtered into a narrative dripping with blood and lust would be simply ridiculous if they weren't so loathsome"[20] Schultze's censure was necessary, he felt, because many people still laughed off colportage as pretty harmless junk.

To the oft-made argument that readers could learn about history and current events by reading colportage, Schultze replied that no knowledge could be acquired from these novels. The historical framework presented was usually inaccurate, characters were given qualities they did not possess in actuality, and even recent events were described with gross factual distortions. Of course, colportage publishers were tremendously skilled at pouncing on current drama and transforming it into an immediate source of lucrative income. An obvious example was the tragic suicide of Austrian Crown Prince Rudolf. According to Schultze, it sparked twenty colportage titles, totaling more than 180,000 copies. Schultze admitted that he too, as a child, had preferred reading about the exciting feats of fictitious Indian chiefs, like White Eagle or Black Bear, despite the efforts of his teachers to make heroes out of Frederick the Great, Bismarck, and generals Moltke and Blücher. He also admitted that young people gripped with Lesewut (reading mania) tended to be more intelligent than those who did not read and instead spent their free time playing cards, drinking beer, or amusing themselves in a variety hall.[21] This was why it was so important to steer these youths away from printed trash towards the great repository of national literary treasures. Schultze claimed to have witnessed the lively interest of school children attending Friedrich Schiller's plays Maria Stuart and William Tell. Although many efforts of this type were made to substitute good literature for bad, the Schundkämpfer actually had little success despite all their concern and agitation. A fundamental reason why they were unable to comprehend the readers of trashy literature was their purist, pietistical approach to reading. This approach descended from a Lutheran tradition that viewed reading as a solemn, serious affair, one meant to lift readers upward to religion, philosophy, and art.[22] In stark contrast, colportage delivered pleasure for readers and profits for publishers. But reading was not supposed to be associated with such profanity.

Picture 4: A boy conspicuously holds his colportage pamphlet in the shadows behind his back. He looks at a poster advertising an exhibition against trashy literature sponsored by the German Writers' Memorial Foundation. Note the well-dressed bourgeois women and men passing by. (Illustration on p.20 in Festschrift der Deutschen Dichter-Gedächtnis-Stiftung zum 10 jährigen Bestehen 1901–1911, *Hamburg, 1912).*

In the war against trashy literature, there were many enemies to be singled out. Most obvious were the colporteurs who "ran up and down the back stairwells in order to deliver their pamphlets to every worker's flat and every servant's room."[23] The German synonym for colportage novel was Hintertreppenroman, literally back staircase novel. You did not have to wait for a colporteur to indulge your appetite. Schund could also be bought in cigar shops and stationery stores (often frequented by school children and students). Pamphlets were hawked by street vendors. Schultze mentions a large colportage distribution center that did not mind selling directly to youths and was owned by a Jew (he thereby reinforced a common prejudice that Jewish merchants in particular profited from this national menace).[24] Publishers were another enemy. They took advantage of modern technology like rotation machines and giant rolls of low quality paper to make profits from their cheap products. Lastly, there were the poorly paid writers who were often called "scribblers" by the Schundkämpfer. Schultze thought it appropriate to compare the low operational costs and high profits of a colportage publishing house to the similar modus_operandi of any house of prostitution.[25]

With so many means of acquisition at the disposal of consumers, how could parents, teachers, employers, and officials be surprised if they witnessed the growing sales of colportage? Whether in a factory, the home of a craftsman or farmer, or in the basket of a servant girl, one could find it. These nefarious pamphlets sometimes seemed to take on a life of their own: "Even in hospitals," asserted Schultze, "they secretly move from bed to bed, disappearing under pillows as soon as the doctor or nurse appears."[26] Happily for the crusaders against trashy literature, the 1911 Reichstag exhibition gained a lot of attention and positive publicity. The sponsors notified everyone that the materials could be boxed up and sent to any city wishing to display them. Schultze was also pleased with increasing local government interventions against Schund. Hamburg revoked newspaper kiosk licenses if the owners sold American-style series like Nick Carter or Buffalo Bill. Hamburg and Leipzig made it illegal to hawk trashy literature in city streets.[27] Württemberg forbade the sale of Nick Carter and Das kleine Witzblatt in train station stores. Prussia went even further forbidding the sale of any trashy literature in train stations.[28]

Sometimes prohibition and pressure groups got embroiled in conflicts with local businesses. A school organization in Berlin called for a boycott of stationery stores selling trashy literature. An organization representing the stores found the declamations calling the owners "businessmen without a conscience" to be unfair and insulting. A similar teachers' boycott in Cottbus made a storekeeper so angry that he put a news article in his display window about a school principal who had been convicted for embezzlement. He added information about a Bautzen teacher sentenced to three years in jail for sex crimes and a teacher in Dörnburg sentenced to death for murder. When a police officer asked about the purpose of such an odd display, he replied that he wanted people to know the truth about the character of the sanctimonious teaching profession which was seeking to ruin his business. A court case resulted in a one hundred marks fine for the store owner because he had insulted teachers. Schultze confidently advised school groups to continue with their boycotts as national law was on their side: since teachers carried a moral responsibility for their students even outside school premises, their actions to defend against Schund were legitimate. Businesses had no chance of winning reparations from teachers who issued boycotts against vendors of trashy literature.[29]

The alliance against trashy literature was broad and powerful. There was nothing that stationery store owners, kiosks, or street vendors could do to protect themselves. The Berlin stores had pointed out that the majority of their Schund customers were adults, but this argument also did not dissuade city officials from taking a hard line. In 1909 an association of publishers distributed a flyer at bookstores entitled "A Word in Defense." Their opponents, colportage publishers argued, "are breathing fire and brimstone so as to besmirch the favorite suspense and entertainment literature of our friends. In our time," they continued, "everything needs to be softened and flattened! Today we need no more romance, no more heroes!"[30] They also attacked newspapers for unanimously opposing colportage. This unity was pure hypocrisy as it aimed simply to eliminate a competitor from the field of mass literature (newspapers included

novels published in daily episodes). Schultze had no sympathy for these
views. He wanted to expand the campaign against trashy literature and
recommended that more towns establish local chapters for monitoring
and curtailing its distribution. These chapters should include not only
local officials, but teachers and representatives from worker unions and
occupational groups. The towns at the forefront of the movement were
Göttingen and Lübeck. They could serve as models for the rest of Germany.

To better understand the source of this cultural conflict one needs to
take a closer look at colportage literature itself. Only by examining the
text can one begin to understand its appeal to a mass of readers, or the
qualities that dismayed the many angry critics. In the rest of this study,
I will examine the novel Das Weib des Ringkämpfers oder Manneskraft
und Frauenherz (hereafter referred to as WRK). I purchased a copy
of the novel from a Berlin antiquarian bookseller in 2020. It may be
the last surviving copy of this novel for there are no copies listed in
the worldwide catalogue of books, nor is there a copy in the large and
unique Günter Kosch Kolportageroman collection in the Deutsches
Literaturarchiv, Marbach.[31] Serial novels were rarely included in library
collections for reasons that are pretty obvious: this was not serious
literature, according to the educated elite, and therefore did not merit
a place in a library. Regional commanders and local governments in
World War I published lengthy lists of colportage titles and called for
them to be "eingestampft" or pulped. For example, in the Offizieller
Anzeiger für Mecklenburg-Strelitz, Number 173 (published November
15, 1917), WRK is book number 220, two positions after the notorious
female detective series Wanda von Brannburg. Many of the listed books
had already been attacked before the war. With pride, Schultze reported
on the positive effects of a 1908 Schundkampf bulletin sent to parents of
Hamburg schoolchildren. Threatened with parental beatings, children
gave up their pamphlets and watched as angry parents burned them in
hearths and ovens.

3. Enter Siegfried the Wrestler

For maximum exposure and in the hope of clinching numerous sub-scriptions, the first installment of a colportage novel was distributed far and wide for free. Writers and publishers knew that if the initial episode failed to ignite interest among the readers, the novel would not take off. Heinrich Büttner, the author of WRK, packed the first episode with action and plenty of violence. The story begins in a Gothic mode. The twelve year-old adopted boy Siegfried accompanies his blacksmith father Sebastian Trutz on a stormy night to a castle. He tries to dissuade his aging parent from a risky endeavor. A female ghost inhabits one of the castle towers. She is actually Siegfried's mother. Her husband, Count von Rüden, had taken the sickly baby Siegfried away from the mother and given it to the blacksmith to raise. This cruel act drove the mother into insanity and she was thereafter locked up in the tower. A healthy baby, Egon, was given to the nobleman as a replacement so he could have a robust, male heir. This child would grow up to be the quintessence of evil and Siegfried's eternal rival. The blacksmith succeeds in scaling the tower. His aim is to have the mother prove that Siegfried is the rightful heir to the family fortune and the title of count. As bad luck would have it, the blacksmith's intrusion causes the mother (who recognizes the unwanted adopter of her child) to have a heart attack. Alarmed castle retainers capture the blacksmith and accuse him of trying to steal the lady's jewelry.

Büttner then shifts events ten years ahead. Siegfried has replaced his foster father as blacksmith at the family foundry located in the forest. He has managed to take care of his little foster sister Hilde. She has

turned into a beautiful woman and gotten the attention of Egon, the im-
poster son of Count von Rüden. Egon's red hair is a colportage signal of
his cursed, evil character and a symbolic negative attribute with deep
roots in folklore and popular literature. Egon pays and instructs an English boxer, Bob Craven, to kidnap Hilde. Dressed as a journeying arti-
san, the English hireling begs Siegfried for an abode for the night. Here
the story intertwines current anti-English animosities within a national-
mythological background. The deceitful Englishman, who is actually a
well-known boxer, takes advantage of the innocent young German's hospitality. His attempt to abduct the blonde girl fails when she calls out for
help. Siegfried comes to the rescue and shows superhuman powers similar to those of his Nibelungen namesake. Armed with a large hammer
made in his own forge, he crushes the perfidious Englishman in a fierce
fight. Siegfried is so outraged by his adversary's cruel plan that even his
supplicating sister cannot prevent him from striking a fatal blow. "No,
don't cry Hilde!" exclaims Siegfried, "I am not a murderer; I have become an avenger of our honor."[1] Wilhelmine colportage did not allow
heroes to kill indiscriminately. There had to be a moral dimension to it: in
this case, the girl's virginity and safety are at stake as well as the family's
honor. Realizing that the police may mistakenly arrest them for murder,
Siegfried and Hilde decide to flee to the city. Siegfried sets fire to home
and foundry, lamenting melodramatically that an old gypsy curse on the
place had finally proven true.

In the city, Siegfried notices a circus poster advertisement. It challenges any man to step forward to win a reward if he can defeat the famed
Turkish wrestler Kara Achmed. Colportage fiction liked to claim that it
was based on reality so it is not surprising that Büttner integrates this
real wrestler into his story. Name recognition was enough, no attempt
was made to draw an accurate portrayal of Achmed. Certainly critics had
a point when they condemned the indiscriminate mixing of fiction and
reality. What makes the description of Achmed particularly egregious
is the fact that it is colored with racial prejudice: "Was this a monster
out of a fairytale? Did Goliath look like this? ...On broad shoulders and
almost without a neck, sat the square head. The face was full of pock
marks and frightfully ugly. A thick black mustache grew above pursed

lips. The deeply recessed eyes revealed a sharp intelligence and expressed unmistakeable cruelty."[2] (This description did not at all fit the real Kara Achmed, a rather handsome man in the photographs of the time.)

No one dares enter the ring to take on the champion wrestler. The circus master of ceremonies asks one last time if anyone will accept the challenge and the possibility of winning a large prize. Finally one man responds. Siegfried steps into the arena, saying "I would like to earn five thousand marks by throwing Kara Achmed."[3] The crowd explodes with cheers of support but expects the giant Turk to dispose quickly of the young German. No colportage writer would countenance the victory of a non-European over a European so the experienced reader anticipates the challenger's triumph. The "surprise win" would find warm approval among many colportage readers who identified themselves with the role of underdog. In a heatedly contested battle, Siegfried boldly uses the technically difficult "wind-mill" maneuver dramatically sweeping his opponent off his feet and then pinning him.[4] The jubilant crowd cries out. Siegfried's glorious first wrestling win turns him into an international celebrity and will be followed by many more.

The hero hardly has time to enjoy his victory when he receives an alarming note from Hilde. She found work as a servant for the Polish Countess Borowska. Another morally corrupt aristocrat, the countess mistreats poor Hilde. Siegfried wants to rescue his sister but he is intercepted by a beautiful brunette named Karla who also appeals for help. She is the countess's stepdaughter and tells Siegfried that, against her will, she has been promised to Kara Achmed in return for a large sum of money. Borowska suffers from the aristocratic disease of compulsive gambling and needs to repay large debts. That both Hilde and Karla are victims of the same evil character is a coincidence typical of colportage. Such unlikely, bizarre plots exasperated bourgeois opponents but did not bother colportage adherents.

Karla helps Siegfried by giving him a key to a balcony door so that he can enter the house unnoticed. For the second time in the narrative he intervenes in the last possible moment to save Hilde's innocence from a lecherous criminal. Borowska and Kara Achmed do not realize that Hilde has taken Karla's place in the bed in order to save her from the terrible Turk. Just as "his muscular arms wrapped themselves around the lovely shape and his lips searched for those of the sleeping girl," Siegfried bursts into the room.[5] "Mädchenschänder! [Girl molester]" thunders Siegfried, "You are not defiling this virgin!"[6] At this point the cliffhanger stops on page twenty-four of the first pamphlet.[7] The illustration at the front of the second pamphlet shows Siegfried gripping his opponent's neck. In the background, Countess Borowska tilts to the side with a look of confusion. Pamphlet number one also depicted a dramatic fight scene elaborating the theme of Siegfried as protector and avenger of the female gender. (See illustrations 1A on p. 99.)

In twenty-four pages Büttner presents a densely packed story with multiple typical colportage themes. First there is the separation and reunion of hero and heroine. Then we have the hero saving the girl's honor from men without scruples. Egon is a corrupt noble. Bob Craven and Kara Achmed are tools of Egon or the equally corrupt noblewoman Borowska. Such conflicts between good and evil are a mainstay of colportage and elaborated in seemingly endless variations within this type of literature. Siegfried, his adoptive father Sebastian Trutz, and Hilde are turned into renegades through no fault of their own. The theme of law enforcement's mistaken quest to arrest the victims instead of the perpetrators of crime is another constantly present colportage theme. According to colportage's populist slant, governments failed to carry out their most solemn task: the provision of true and equal justice for all. This is connected to the question of whether or not the hero has the right to take justice into his own hands, even to the point of killing criminals.

Extreme turns of fate, like Siegfried's penniless entrance to the city and subsequent richness from the prize money for throwing Kara Achmed, characterize colportage plots and give the readers the thrill of vicariously experiencing the main character's cycles of rise and fall. Finally, Büttner created a web of character interrelationships that would grow into greater complexity as the narrative continues over the course of thousands of pages. Keeping the story straight would be a challenge for the readers and sometimes for the authors themselves. Oral group reading of a serial novel held the advantage that members could remind each other or discuss who did what, when, and where. If necessary, one could always refer back to a previous episode to clarify a point or discover a sloppy mistake or contradiction. Sometimes authors lost oversight due to their enormous and rapid literary output (or because multiple authors were at work).

4. Wrestling

An interesting aspect of WRK is that Büttner uses the increasingly popular "sport" of wrestling to organize his sprawling novel. By the late nineteenth century, wrestling had gained the attention of large audiences in Europe and North America. The raw confrontation of brute force coupled with athletic skill excited a public with an insatiable appetite for entertainment and sensation. In an age when fledgling team and individual sports recruited more and more athletes and enthusiastic spectators, the question of rules and their application by referees and officials became an ongoing challenge. Wrestling would be a particularly vexing form of athleticism because it had a poor reputation on account of its origins in amusement parks or fairground sideshows and the numerous incidences of indecorous violence, bloodshed, and even death. On top of its perceived vulgarity, wrestling quickly gained notoriety for rigged matches, a problem further complicated by betting scandals. While major wrestling matches and tournaments received much media attention, accompanying critical news articles were also often filled with accusations of malfeasance. All this notwithstanding, the spectacle of wrestling gained enormous popularity in the decades preceding World War I. Some entrepreneurs sensed that a large part of the audience "did not want straight wrestling – they wanted a 'show' and a 'show' they were given."[1]

Picture 5: Around the turn-of-the-century, international wrestling tournaments became increasingly popular and featured wrestlers like Heinrich Eberle, winner of "the Golden Belt of Frankfurt" on April 22, 1907 (Postcard 1907).

Certainly Büttner's WRK was an original, attention-gaining device in the competitive market for colportage readers and new subscriptions. For the historian of popular culture, colportage's utilization of wrestling as a theme reveals a clever strategy by one form of mass entertainment exploiting the popularity of another. Büttner's novel's title did not completely fulfill its promise. The fan of wrestling who subscribed probably would have been disappointed by the relatively few scenes of actual wrestling presented in the novel, nor was there much to increase the reader's knowledge of the sport's milieu or fine points about training or the use of various moves and holds. Büttner did ably manage, however, to place the bouts of his hero within the scheme of competing, contrasting national imageries and identities. The wrestler Siegfried is an incarnation of German physical invincibility coupled with a character of impeccable honesty. This convergence of sheer strength, athletic dexterity, and virtue made him a powerful fictional source of national inspiration and identification.

The wrestling arena could also provide a litmus test where racial encounters revealed the author's level of prejudice. Siegfried's first match with the famous Turkish wrestler is a demonstration not only of the white man's physical prowess and superiority, but in the fight that happens shortly after the match, the moral force of the European defeats the wickedness of his non-European rival. The novel's second illustration shows Siegfried with Kara Achmed in his grasp. The bulging eyes of the Turk and his not quite human countenance have their "artistic" roots in a racial propagandistic tradition that goes all the way back to the sixteenth century paintings of Turkish-Christian battles that portray Turkish soldiers as inhuman demons.

A match against the black American wrestler Redgrey offers the public the particularly "spicy appeal" of seeing who is stronger: black or white. The giant black wrestler is considerably taller and heavier than Siegfried, yet Redgrey soon realizes that his sheer size alone will not subdue the German. The black man falls to the speed and dexterity of his smaller adversary. A "fanatic applause" courses through the white spectators, while an angry grumbling spreads among the black audience. A racial battle is averted by the menacing stance of the white spectators which causes the fearful blacks to retreat. Although Siegfried's victories over the black American and the Turk are supposed to symbolize white superiority, Büttner distinguishes his hero's attitude towards black people from crude American racism. A young lady of New Orleans tells Siegfried that white Americans consider black Americans to be creatures lower than animals. Siegfried contradicts her: "I think a black man and a white are the same. A black man deserves respect if he acts like a gentleman."[2] This, however, is not the case with Redgrey, who practices the lowest forms of skulduggery.

Picture 6: The competitors in Hannover's 1905 Wrestling Championship included two black men. Wrestling was an inclusive, global sport and the focus of international media attention (Postcard 1905).

Wintergarten Hannover —— II. grosse internationale Ringkampf-Konkurrenz 1905.

Wrestling competitions, in WRK, do not always portend personal conflicts. Siegfried faces the white American champion Bob Simons in New York. The reader is told that Americans have tremendous respect for wrestlers and boxers. Their incomes can reach as high as one hundred thousand dollars for a single victory. Even people of the highest public office openly show their admiration for great athletes, putting them on the same level as important intellectual or cultural figures. Siegfried is pleasantly surprised to find that his adversary is not the typical "rough plebeian" but a blonde gentleman similar to himself. This man has depth of character and quickly becomes a friend to Siegfried. The match between the respected colleagues, nevertheless, reverberates with intercontinental rivalry: "It was as if a battle between Old and New World was about to take place. Would young America crush old Europe, or would the representative of America lie at Europe's feet?"[3]

The contest begins. Both wrestlers employ all the moves of the wrestling repertoire as they try to overcome their opponent. When Siegfried is in trouble, he is described as standing as firm as the trunk of an oak, the national tree of Germany. During a short pause, Siegfried ensures his manager that everything is under control. Again, it is Siegfried's lightning speed that makes the difference as he finally pins the American. At the match's climax, the huge crowd is on its feet, brimming over with ecstatic excitement. After the whistle of the referee marks the match's end, the crowd "howls, screams, stamps its feet" and cheers the European victor in a fair and unprejudiced manner.[4] The two wrestlers embrace and Siegfried courteously declares that his opponent was his equal and the best wrestler he ever faced. Such chivalry goes over well with the spectators who honor both men with long cheers.

Büttner's overall positive assessment of the American crowd contrasts with a contemporary newspaper description of conditions in the Anglo-American wrestling world: "While the Germans remain calm and cool, the word 'sport' has an electric effect on the English and Americans. Sport, for Germans, is a game or entertainment, or a means for improving physical strength or health. One does not give a sport event half the serious attention or enthusiasm that England or America give it. Some people think that the Berliners interest in the currently hosted wrestling matches is extraordinary, yet it is hardly worth mentioning when compared to the excitement celebrated in an American city that hosts a prizefight. Americans are enthralled where raw power shows itself and if some blood flows, so much the better."[5] The reporter notes that a prize boxer can achieve national fame in America. Germans, in contrast, find boxing's raw brutality disgusting. The writer first argues that outrageous financial prizes for boxing or wrestling would never be offered in Berlin's competitions, but then reconsiders when describing the current 1905 tournament organized by former champion Jakob Koch.

Picture 7: Jakob Koch became heavy-weight world champion in Greco-Roman wrestling in 1902 and 1904. H. Eberle was one of the wrestlers he defeated in 1904. Unlike Siegfried, Koch trained methodically and also organized competitions (Postcard 1903).

In a discussion with a nobleman, Siegfried explains that wrestling can be a lucrative source of income. He sometimes makes two thousand pounds for a single match.[6] The international attention given to the greatest wrestlers, their status as global celebrities, could indeed engender sums of money unseen in previous times when strongmen were relegated to a fairground booth, competing with magic shows or displays of colonial dancers. Siegfried's professionalism manifests itself in his abstinence from alcohol and tobacco. When he throws the giant Calabrian Ezardo, he tells the astonished audience that his opponent, despite his size, could never succeed as a wrestler because of his drinking habits. Physical training or warm-up preparation for a match is, however, never mentioned in the novel (Leroy, Siegfried's manager, does recommend taking walks). Siegfried's prowess, the reader learns, is due to a combination of attitude, discipline, and an inborn ability or gift.

Even the tsar of Russia wants to enjoy watching the acclaimed star in competition with his own mighty wrestler Kanzurow. Like Ezardo, the Russian has a fatal weakness for alcohol. Siegfried's manager informs him that the famed Kanzurow no longer consumes vodka, but, on account of his great wealth, prefers expensive wines, champagnes, and liqueurs, "...you know Siegfried that someone who indulges in sport cannot enjoy too much alcohol."[7] Yet, before the match, the tsar warns Siegfried that the Russian wrestler is capable of uprooting trees. Siegfried calmly replies, "Your Majesty, if I may say so, wrestling is not all about strength. More important are dexterity and the speedy ability to choose the right move at the right time..."[8] Tsar Nicholas is impressed by the young German's confidence. His deputy then shows Siegfried the diamond-studded, engraved gold chain that the empress will bestow on the winner. The fight fulfills all expectations. At first it seems that the Russian's enormous strength will overpower Siegfried just as the emperor predicted. The skilled German, however, manages to extricate himself from a dangerous hold and with suppleness throws and pins the Russian. The amazed tsar applauds, declaring Siegfried "the greatest wrestler in the world" and adds that the German not only fought brilliantly but also fairly.[9] Such accolades, coming from one of the world's most powerful monarchs, were inserted in the text for a purpose. The indomitable hero once more serves as a fictional device to heighten the reader's sense of national pride. Siegfried is invincible and a man of perfect virtue. In him, German power fuses with ethical superiority.

Towards the novel's end, Siegfried is challenged to wrestle George Hackenschmidt (in actuality, considered the world's finest wrestler at the turn-of-the-century). The French entrepreneur Leroy, who manages Siegfried, is genuinely worried about this match because of Hacken-schmidt's undefeated record. In fact, he did not lose a single match between 1898 and 1908. Most of these were fought in the Greco-Roman style popular on the European continent. He also won numerous catch-as-catch-can matches which were preferred in England and the United States. Büttner never dwells on such technicalities. Although he deftly describes Siegfried's bouts so as to heighten suspense and excitement, it is not his aim to present well-researched or accurate details about wrestling. What matters is holding the reader's attention, not educating him or her. Feelings always count for more in colportage than knowledge or thought. When Leroy asks, with some concern, if Siegfried is worried about the upcoming challenge, the wrestler replies, "I don't think about it. I just feel that I will be victorious."[10] The competition never takes place because Hackenschmidt cancels. Siegfried reflects that his rival's long and great career is coming to an end and he prefers not humiliating the famed Russian athlete. Instead, he competes in an invitational international tournament in Berlin where he prevails over everyone and is crowned world champion.

5. National and Ethnic Stereotypes

While Büttner wastes no time describing the training that would have been realistically needed by a successful wrestler, he does focus on the need for an impresario who can skillfully promote the career of a celebrity wrestler. That he chose to give the role to the Frenchman Charles Leroy is no coincidence. Profitable careers in wrestling were in fact managed mainly by French, English, or American entrepreneurs. Siegfried's talents and good looks get promoted by a character who becomes a wise and trustworthy friend. Historian Mark Hewitson, in Germany and the Modern World 1880–1914 , observes that France was Germany's traditional "mentor and teacher."[1] Symbolically, the narrative of WRK shows how Franco-German cooperation can be mutually beneficial. Of course the ties between a Frenchman and a German cannot completely avoid the shadows of the past. When Siegfried tells Leroy that he wants to settle down in Berlin, Leroy explains he cannot live there on account of the humiliating treaty inflicted on France in 1870–1871.[2]

Notwithstanding such frictions, Leroy is described as "fatherly friend."[3] He repeatedly warns Siegfried of his inclination to get entangled in dangerous amorous relations. Illustration 93 shows a busy café scene, Leroy and Siegfried are seated at a table where a pretty young woman catches Siegfried's eye. (See illustration 93 on p. 104). Mysteriously dressed in a widow's outfit, she looks at Siegfried with melancholy eyes. He is all attention while Leroy gazes at the viewer seemingly saying, "Here we go again!" Throughout the novel, Leroy's faithful and trustworthy behavior benefits the German athlete and it seems like Leroy himself has no other person to whom he is attached. But Büttner reveals in a sub-narrative entitled "Leroy's Wound in the Heart" that the Frenchman once had an ill-fated romance with a woman named Daisy. He met her in the scandal-plagued Moulin Rouge nightclub. The reader is told about Leroy's visits to the notorious home of the cancan dance: "There is nothing more beautiful in all of Paris than this wild confusion, these lightning flashes in the eyes, this crazy passion, this mania, this bacchanalian dance!"[4] Along with sensual excitement comes moral compromise. In participating in the Moulin Rouge's merrymaking one sells one's soul to the devil. This is Leroy's own point of view. So why is he there? Büttner comments that Leroy is only an observer – which absolves him a bit. When Leroy sees a young woman tired of dancing he invites her to his table. In a fatherly way, he admonishes her for visiting this disreputable place. She agrees to leave with her new protector.

The friendship soon evolves into a romantic relationship that fills Leroy with joy. Before long, the couple plans to marry. All would seem normal were it not for a strange problem. At a certain time every evening, Diana calls for a carriage to take her home. She always makes sure that Leroy cannot follow her. The mysterious nightly departures drive Leroy to desperation. Here the author Büttner risked offending a part of his readership. He has Leroy comment that Diana clearly came from a good family background and not from the lower classes that one would expect to frequent shady nightclubs. Diana is neither a factory worker nor a servant girl. Besides offending these female groups, Büttner also applies a typical turn-of-the-century double standard. While a young bourgeois woman has no business frequenting a place like the Moulin Rouge, a bourgeois man, like Leroy, can visit a place of ill-repute for a little amusement.

At the end of this story within a story, which also functions as a cautionary tale, a gravely disappointed Leroy discovers that Diana is actually the inmate of an insane asylum who escapes to enjoy a few hours of freedom every night. A heartbroken Leroy learns that the young woman is incurably ill. She forcefully resists being locked in the asylum by her family, calling out "do you hear the music? It's the cancan from the Moulin Rouge, oh how sweet!"[5] A sadly disillusioned Leroy explains to his friend Siegfried that it is through this affair that he learned an important lesson: "I have become more tranquil since then. I no longer sought out such places where one can experience so-called adventures."[6] The bitter lesson for Leroy is that a true romance culminating in bourgeois matrimony cannot possibly begin in a sultry Parisian nightclub. Büttner's typical moralizing colportage paternalism reveals itself in this denouement.

Danger and degeneration characterize not only the Moulin Rouge. Leroy warns his charge that, in a world city like Paris, danger lurks everywhere. Siegfried promises his mentor that he spends most of his time strolling out in the Bois de Boulogne, enjoying the fresh air. Elegant ladies promenade out there but Siegfried knows to avoid them. He also avoids the new fad of drinking absinthe in a coffeehouse at 5 pm., and he does not attend the theater or frequent dancehalls.

With all this caution one suspects Siegfried may actually make his next wrestling appointment, organized by his manager, and not be sidetracked by another amorous adventure. Colportage, though, has its own logic and a new trap snaps shut on poor Siegfried. He has been mistaken for his evil foster brother Egon von Rüden. The latter had slyly taken a recruitment premium from the French Foreign Legion but absconded shortly after enlisting. Siegfried is captured and brought to the Paris headquarters, making a futile plea that he is not the culprit. He also insists that the Kaiser will not allow any of his subjects to be mistreated.[7] Such proclamations are ignored as Siegfried is packed off on a ship sailing for Algeria.

Whereas Paris is depicted in all of its unique French glory, the Foreign Legion shows a darker side to France. Conditions are rough, mortality rates high. The sub-plot turns into one more of Siegfried's adventures and it also functions as another cautionary tale. Through the hero's hardships, the reader ponders why "some warm tears have been spilled over there in faraway Africa by those who left the homeland."[8] Siegfried is determined to escape the legion as soon as possible. First, though, he is locked in a battle with the Berbers. He saves his unit's flag and then kills the young Berber leader, noting with pathos that he was a handsome and noble man.[9] Siegfried does not question or think about why colonial forces battle indigenous people. His behavior is quite simple: "I just did my duty."[10] To deflect any criticism from the novel's hero, in a completely unrealistic scene, the fallen Berber's father forgives Siegfried and even awards him with his fallen son's sword. Siegfried is moved by this gesture and says he will never forget the old man's nobility.

While, at least, the Berbers are described in a positive way, Büttner lets the reader know that it is the job of the colonial power to put the African territory to good use. France plans to build a canal from the Mediterranean Sea into the Sahara, thereby transforming the desert into a vast sea. No explanation is given as to how this will benefit anyone but it is implied that it is part of an inexorable process of applying technology for the sake of progress. So the romanticized Berbers need to be brushed aside by the forces of a superior, scientifically advanced civilization.

Colonized people, however, do not always get to bask in the dusk light of a vanishing Orient. When Siegfried and Leroy travel to America they come into contact with Chinese culture in San Francisco. Equipped with revolvers, Leroy warns that wherever Chinese people live, there is a lot of crime: "For the Chinese are a strange people and have a peculiar character."[11] Gambling is their biggest vice: "The Mongolians cannot overcome the gambling craze because it is in their blood."[12] Visiting a Chinese restaurant, Leroy comments in a derogatory fashion about Chinese foods. They eat such disgusting things as baked mealworms and cooked entrails of rats. (He does admit, however, that their tea is superior to that of the Europeans.) Büttner also makes derogatory physical comparisons by having Leroy say that the Chinese remind him of cats and monkeys.

Needless to say, the Chinese represent a threat and Siegfried pays a heavy price when he innocently volunteers to take part in a magic show's disappearing act. He ends up locked in a trunk. Once more, evil Egon is behind it all. Seeking revenge for the fact that Siegfried called him a bastard and repeated the claim that he was not the real Count von Rüden, Egon pays a Chinese magician to trick and trap the wrestler. A young woman persuades Egon to put the trunk on a China-bound ship filled with coffins and Chinese corpses. She later has a change of heart, boards the ship, and bribes the guards to release the prisoner from the trunk.

Büttner also reveals prejudices when he describes American Indians as savages who wish to see the blood of whites.[13] They are wild and cruel. Their hatred, the author notes, is understandable when one considers that their hunting grounds have been taken. The white people either want the Indians dead or pushed into reservations. Siegfried, Leroy, and Hilde are captured by a band of Delaware Indians. Their plan is to burn the white trio at the stake, but the young chief Eagle Feather cancels all this when he falls in love with Hilde and wants to marry her. Hilde explains to him that a white woman cannot marry "a redskin."[14] Leroy than hatches a plan in which Hilde will pretend to go along with the chief's wishes. The night of the wedding she will stab him to death and the three will escape. This will all be made easier by the fact, Leroy predicts with certainty, that the American Indians will get roaring drunk.

The wedding day arrives. The three captive Europeans observe the wanton excess of the Indians as they consume alcohol and gorge themselves on food. Their dance "seems infernal."[15] Siegfried and Leroy patiently watch the wedding celebration and spend time discussing whether it is even possible for a white European and an American Indian to fall in love. The color barrier prevents it, claims Siegfried, but Leroy does not share this opinion and tells of a case where a white man and an American Indian woman genuinely fell in love. Such views show that Büttner employed standard racial clichés and prejudices, but also made reservations, sometimes challenging all-out racism.

Several times the topic of money-lending and Jewry comes up. One of Büttner's characters, an Italian nobleman, explains that Christian usurers do not behave better than Jewish ones.[16] (For Büttner's prejudiced portrayal of Jews in an 1892 novel see the postscript). In another episode, a profligate officer has to deal with an unpleasant, pushy moneylender and it is noted that he "is not a Hebrew, but a very pious Christian."[17] Contrasting this tolerant viewpoint, one of the novel's illustrators drew a standard antisemitic caricature of a Jew that reinforced the popular imagery of Jews as overbearing schemers (see illustration 79 on p. 121). The role of Jews, however, in the novel is minor. Far more exciting and diabolical are the American Indians.

After Siegfried's mentor Leroy argues that a romance between a white person and an American Indian is possible, he quickly adds that an American Indian's capacity to love rarely attains the sublime levels achieved by white people: "...When using these words, one cannot equate [the American Indian's feelings] to the beautiful, deep, heartfelt, and poetic sensibility known by the whites. Only in the rarest cases is the love of an Indian true and noble. Usually it is only an arousal of the senses or the animal instincts... that attracts him to a woman."[18] Turn-of-the-century racial and colonial ideology tended to make this distinction between a European capacity to enter ideal, ethereal spheres of the sublime, and the inferior, animal nature of the non-Europeans. Still, here too, Büttner's racial arguments allow for exceptions and possible convergences that hard-baked brands of racism would repudiate. For example, Siegfried's willingness to respect a black man of honor had been contrasted by a white Southerner's absolute intolerance and fierce racism.[19]

In general, Americans do not have a positive image in WRK. The United States is a country of extremes and excess. On the one hand, there is great wealth and the success of the self-made man, on the other, many Americans live in poverty. The robber barons are rich, but their achievement in building railroads and banks can be traced back to all sorts of immorality, notably corruption, deceit, and even murder.[20] Siegfried holds an oft-repeated view that Americans judge everything according to its monetary value. American millionaires purchase great art not because they appreciate it but because they want to show off.[21] Materialism rules America. Germans, in contrast, have depth and soul. When German male immigrants arrive in the New World they cannot find adequate female companions. A German immigrant scorns American women because "they like to flirt and take it too far."[22]

Americans are filled with hypocrisy. Continually trumpeting freedom, they are actually intolerant conformists: "On Sunday you cannot find a drop of beer or alcohol, a theater performing a play, or... an open dancehall."[23] A land of stark contrasts, America is also a place where man's raw and brutal instincts find release, not just among American Indians but among white Europeans as well.[24] About the only good thing Büttner says about Americans is that sports audiences are fair and will cheer a foreigner even if he defeats an American. The novel's anti-Americanism has a cautionary function – warning its readers that they may be disappointed should they join the millions of emigrants who departed for America expecting a land of milk and honey. This critical standpoint did not prevent WRK's marketing among Germans in the USA. The Deutscher Herold of Sioux Falls offered the complete novel at a discount price of three dollars and, along with other serial novels, advertised it as "exciting reading for long, winter evenings."[25] The emigrant newspaper also recommended that three or four readers band together so as to make orders more affordable.[26]

WRK reflects and reinforces many common national stereotypes of the late nineteenth and early twentieth centuries. Curiously, very little is said about Germany's great rival, England. Only in the first few pages does the kidnapper Bob Craven reveal "typical" English deceit and treachery. In London, Siegfried defeats the great English wrestler Munroe and is congratulated by the attending Prince of Wales. Leroy is ecstatic and admits that he was worried about the match since England boasts some of the world's best wrestlers. Siegfried's reply contains a message for the German reader: one need not fear the English, with focused willpower they can be defeated. "Surely, he is enormously strong and as mobile as a snake," the wrestler sizes up, "but I had resolved to win, and when one is inspired by a decision, then there is no one on earth who can throw me."[27]

Even when Siegfried is on the verge of dying, his calm self-control exudes a courage that is supposedly typically German.[28] This is "proven" in two episodes where Siegfried has been mistakenly sentenced to death. About to use the guillotine, a French executioner admires Siegfried's stoicism while awaiting his demise. An Italian bandit who plans to kill his German captive proclaims: "The Germans are brave. I have always liked them."[29] This sort of construed recognition from various nationalities also worked to boost the reader's self-image and increase his or her sense of identification with the German nation. Siegfried thus becomes a symbol for everything good about Germany. The tsarina, herself a German, witnesses his victory over the Russian wrestler and admits that Siegfried makes her proud to be German.[30]

Russia occupied a prominent role in German serial novels because it was a perfect stage for melodrama. The Russian Revolution of 1905 manifested the simmering conflict in this quintessentially patriarchal society. Extremes of wealth and poverty played into the hands of colportage writers who loved to narrate stories of personal rise and fall, of arrest by secret police, banishment to Siberia, and then an adventure-filled escape. Büttner could not resist exploiting this type of scenario for his novel.

After his triumphant match before the Tsar, Siegfried finds himself in deep trouble on account of an attractive female terrorist whom he has befriended. The secret police believe Siegfried was part of a plot to assassinate the tsar. Far from it, Siegfried actually held great respect for the world's most powerful monarch and patriarch. Siegfried told Leroy that "he has a benevolent look and I believe he really means it."[31] Like most colportage heroes, Siegfried supports patriarchy – it transposes the holy concept of family into the system of politics and governance.

Yet Leroy has a queasy feeling in Russia, "I don't know. Death lingers in the air. This poor tsar and his entire court are continually in danger and I don't want us to be exposed to this."[32] The troubles are confirmed by the assassination of the Russian Minister of the Interior (which actually happened on July 28, 1904 – but this date does not fit in with the novel's own chronology).[33] The tsarina interprets this act of violence as "a terrible omen."[34] She and her husband regret the departure of Siegfried but he cannot prolong his visit for "he longs for Germany, for my German homeland! Soon I will again see the German oak forests, it is so beautiful in the homeland – so beautiful!"[35] Shortly before the departure for Germany, Livia the enchantingly pretty terrorist, appears begging Siegfried to hide her. He makes the fateful mistake of sheltering her and soon finds himself under arrest in the notorious Peter and Paul Fortress. Büttner rhetorically asks his readers if they have heard of this place, the scariest of Russian prisons, "a hell on earth."[36]

The tsar would like to pardon Siegfried, but personal intrigues in the court prevent it. The trial is a sensation as both "Red Livia" and "Siegfried the Wrestler" take the stand. Livia's guilt is easily proven since she has taken part in previous plots to overthrow the tsar. She is sentenced to death by hanging. Courageously, she upholds Siegfried's innocence and declares he knew nothing of her political tactics. Livia is the only figure in the novel with a clear political position. She is prepared for the ultimate sacrifice and tells Siegfried: "The people will rise up and break their chains. The time is not far off."[37]

Siegfried explains that he came to Russia "in full confidence of Russian hospitality."[38] His lawyer warns the court that if Siegfried is found guilty, Russia's reputation abroad will suffer: "A people who does not hold firm to justice, does not deserve to exist."[39] In the last possible moment, Siegfried receives an imperial order that commutes the death penalty into ten years imprisonment in Siberia. On his way there he manages to find an opportunity to escape. There is plenty of excitement, peppered with violence, and the reader is reminded to appreciate the tranquility, the judicial fairness, and governmental efficiency that contrasts peaceful Germany with turbulent, violent Russia.

6. Current Events and Sensation

One of the favorite topics that colportage writers liked to incorporate in their giant rambling novels was a sensational current event. The murder of the Serbian King Alexander and Queen Draga on July 10, 1903 was exactly the kind of melodrama that serial novelists were ready to exploit. Siegfried, after his Russian adventure, is making his way through the Balkans back to Germany. He stops in Belgrade for a wrestling match that Leroy has arranged. In attendance are the royal family, including the stunning beauty, Queen Draga.[1] She and her husband, King Alexander, are despised by most Serbs. Siegfried and Leroy hear about possible plots to kill the royal couple. "Such a crime would be reprehensible in any case," Siegfried observes, "regicide is one of the most abhorrent transgressions."[2] Leroy offers his contrary, dialectical view. The court is corrupt, a physiognomic glance at the king reveals his inadequacy, and the people may have no other choice for getting rid of the incompetent couple. Leroy's populism rebuffs Siegfried's paternalism. Colportage's disguised politics somehow sought a synthesis of these contradicting positions. This tension persists throughout the novel and the genre in general.

Siegfried makes short shrift of the Serbian wrestler much to the crowd's astonishment and amusement. He even allows himself the luxury of a cigarette after his new victory. Nor can he resist a mysterious invitation from a secret admirer. It is, of course, Draga, whose "hypnotic eyes no man can resist."[3] Draga is quite clever because she is not just interested in a flirt but would like Siegfried as a bodyguard in dangerous times. Siegfried learns that Draga is not really at fault for her bad public image and that she is married to a "nearly insane man."[4]

Picture 8: *The colportage novel* Königin Draga, das Verhängnis von Serbien *(1903–1904) tried to exploit the execution of the monarchs within weeks of the event. It was published by Weichert Verlag of Berlin, one of the largest colportage publishers.*

Büttner portrays Draga as a sort of Cinderella figure. Inaccurately, he describes how she rose from "the salt of the earth" to become a queen. This fairytale setting was meant to beguile readers of such stories, but also to make them think that maybe it was better to be a humble person instead of royalty constantly in danger of assassination. Things heat up when Siegfried cannot resist a kiss just as Alexander enters the queen's boudoir. The king declares he will have them both executed. At the same time the palace revolt begins. The leader is Colonel Maschin, the brother of Draga's first husband. For the sake of simplicity and moving the action along, Büttner condenses the story and thereby grossly distorts the facts. It was exactly these distortions that Schundkämpfer considered to be a flaw of installment novels and a major disservice to their many readers.

In the chaos of revolution, Siegfried is overlooked. For once not a hero, he peeks through a keyhole to witness the "gruesome bloody scene" as the queen is stabbed to death.[5] He also watches and condemns the defenestration of the royal couple. This is done to prove to the public that the revolt is successful. "So he had become witness to this historical event, one of the most baneful that ever took place," the narrator explains.[6] Colonel Maschin finds the time to give his version of the palace revolt to Siegfried in the hope that the German wrestler will defend him in the eyes of history.[7] Siegfried returns to his hotel in a daze and wonders if "the murder of beautiful Queen Draga" had just been "a terrible, bloody dream."

As noted above, colportage critics were exasperated and incensed by this sort of mixing of fact and fiction. They felt young or uneducated readers would take everything at face value, blindly believing the nonsense fed to them. Taking a tragic event like the Serbian regicide and transforming it into sensational literature not only misinformed the public but also exploited the tragedy simply for financial profit. Certainly, when one examines colportage titles, the dramatic, violent fall of royalty or famous people was a favorite theme of the industry and a key to its popular success.

The Belgrade regicide spawned the immediate publication of two colportage novels: Königin Draga, das Verhängnis von Serbien oder der Königsmord von Belgrad (Queen Draga, the Fate of Serbia or Belgrade

Regicide, 1903–1904) and Die Abenteuerin auf dem Königsthron (The Adventurer on the Royal Throne, 1903–1904). How this event captured the popular imagination is further illustrated by contemporary fairground postcards depicting sideshows of reenactments of the royal couple's bloody death. Wax or cardboard figures were filled with "blood" and then decapitated – the "blood" flowed abundantly onto the stage and dripped down from it. The gruesome spectacle took considerable liberty with the facts for the royal couple was stabbed, not decapitated, but this distortion could hardly have affected an audience's attraction to such sensations. Displaying the bleeding, severed heads, was the climax of these sideshow performances.

It is likely that these macabre sideshows earned additional income by selling or having an accompanying, enterprising colporteur sell the novels dedicated to the event. The Vorwärts reported about Johanna Gartz, a young factory worker, who bought a copy of Königin Draga at a county fair and was so captivated by the story she read it into the night. As she succumbed to sleep, she inadvertently knocked over the bedside candle and ended up hospitalized with severe burns. Alas, such outcomes were to be expected from obsessed colportage readers, the admonitory article implied.[8]

Pictures 9: and 10: Sideshows at county fairs reenacted the execution of Serbia's Draga and Alexander. The gory spectacle of decapitation (with fake blood dripping from severed wax or cardboard heads) drew voyeuristic attention from spectators at Langensalza's Jahnplatz fairground (Postcard stamped 1906) and Dresden's Vogelwiese (Postcard stamped 1908).

In another hostile, anti-colportage article, a reader expressed outrage that "the blood had hardly dried" in Serbia when someone exploited the tragedy to create "a novel." The reader saw the book's illustrations in a display window and commented that they were "as bad as always – incredibly crude and foolish."[9] The angry reader's letter and commentary was used by the Vorwärts to note that "they touched a sore point of popular life." The problem was that too many common folk were subjected to "the poisoning and mind-numbing" effects of trashy literature, like the serial novel Königin Draga. With dismay, the Vorwärts complained that, in particular, servant girls, factory women, and young workers, "fled into these childish and bloody horror stories" to escape the "gray misery and monotony of their uneventful lives." The political damage was immense because these readers were "lost to the battles of the modern proletariat, where lucid minds are required."[10] The conundrum continued to vex the SPD as it sought unsuccessfully to make Marx and working class literature more appealing than stories about the murdered Queen Draga.

Another current event Büttner could not resist incorporating in his giant 1907 novel was the San Francisco earthquake of April 18, 1906. Only two days after the earthquake, one of Germany's most reputable newspapers, the Vossische Zeitung, explained the probable origins of the natural disaster in an article entitled "Volcanic and Non-Volcanic Earthquakes."[11] The author observed that the violent eruption of Mount Vesuvius on April 7, 1906 should not be connected with events in California eleven days later. This was a popular mistake. He then explained that earthquakes were caused either by volcanic activity or tectonic movements in the earth's crust.

Only a few earthquake stations registered and charted tremors in 1906. This information was fundamental to developing scientific explanations of the phenomenon. Shifting parts of the earth's crust created tectonic earthquakes most often in mountain chains. The western portion of the U.S. seemed to be particularly prone to such activity. Tectonic movement built mountains and was the most likely cause for the San Francisco disaster. Although geologists could not give a more detailed explanation, their paradigm showed a considerable understanding of the phenomenon. (Alfred Wegener's first book on the origin of continents would be published in 1915.)

Did WRK profit from and build on these scientific views presented in the newspapers? Büttner introduced a new fictional character to the narrative: Professor Louis A. Reymond, head of the Parisian astronomical observatory.[12] This eccentric French professor is more a prophet of doom than a scientist. In his calculations, a global apocalypse will begin in San Francisco. He has come from Paris to witness the great catastrophe and warns his French compatriot to leave the city within twenty-four hours. Reymond explains that the city is precariously located at the top of an underwater mountain.

The professor had met with ridicule after publishing an article in a French paper predicting that the city's demise would be the start of a chain of events in which the world breaks apart. Siegfried also finds the old man's views laughable, "…the city should disappear under sea level – it looks like the poor man really did study too much!" But Leroy takes the professor seriously and unfolds his own dark theory asking how humanity can resist "the secret powers of nature that continually work to obliterate us."[13] He believes in a cyclical rhythm of creation and destruction from which there is no escape. This is all too much pessimism for Siegfried to digest. He protests and his friend agrees to change the subject. Leroy wishes to give the wrestler a tour of San Francisco, starting with fabled Chinatown.

As mentioned earlier, Siegfried is lured into participating in a magic show that turns out to be a trap. He is kidnapped and imprisoned on a boat carrying coffins and corpses to China. Freed by a female admirer, Siegfried reaches the ship's deck just in time to see the great city tumble and fall. He "saw violent columns of fire flaring up all over the city."[14] In shock, Siegfried calls out, "The French professor was right! The end of our days has arrived!"[15] Siegfried's sober, down-to-earth way of viewing reality is wrong, while Leroy's and Professor Reymond's apocalyptic frame of mind is right. Colportage liked to promote this sort of anti-establishment, anti-rational explanation for events. The theory of "eternal return" and "cycles of destiny" included an admonition to a mankind disrespectful of the great forces hidden away in an impenetrable, morally rigorous beyond. Once the thin veneer of civilization is pealed aside, mankind reveals itself as wild and beastly. Büttner describes horrible behavior in the stricken city as everyone thinks only of themselves and their own survival in the inferno. Colportage novels preached biblically that people got what they deserved: "Now lightning flashed down from the skies and the earth quaked in order to destroy the city of vice and sin. Just like long ago Sodom and Gomorrah, so here too: the innocent must perish along with the guilty."[16] This terrible drama was framed by a merciless form of holy terror. Although colportage novelists never elaborated a political position, they created an ideology that could be read between the lines: be chaste and humble; don't rock the boat; accept the role "destiny" has assigned you; do not aspire to change the social order; do not believe in the false promises of science, progress, or socialism. It was a peculiar synthesis of patriarchal conservatism and populism, a complete rejection of nineteenth century liberalism and socialism. Science and reason were rejected in favor of occultism and anti-establishment border sciences.

Linked to these beliefs were what some scholars of nineteenth century literature call the melodramatic mode of perceiving the rapidly changing world. Elaine Hadley, in her Melodramatic Tactics (1995), sees the English audiences of mid-century theater as "threatened by atomization and the resultant disintegration of communal values."[17] What people long for is a family where individual moral behavior follows the guidance of a benevolent patriarch. Social tensions are defused by sentimental bonds and cooperation. Hadley notes the elusiveness of this popular ideology: "Always a hybrid, the melodramatic mode rarely existed in any text or setting in an ideologically pure form; for this very reason, it can only be seen as a rhetorical and performative mode, not a fully realized and internally consistent ideology."[18]

7. Class Conflict: Siegfried as Peacemaker

In WRK the future father-in-law of Siegfried is a wealthy Berlin factory owner. When he discovers that his daughter Bertha loves the famous wrestler and wants to marry him, he is shocked and tells her he does not want a son-in-law who is merely a sideshow strongman. He wishes that Bertha marries a professor or a Prussian officer. Eventually he gives in to her desire on the condition that Siegfried abandons his career and joins the family business. Siegfried agrees but is skeptical about his ability to work at a desk: "It is not in my nature to weigh and calculate, to make long considerations, to press an advantage out of someone else that might not be justified."[1] Siegfried does not mean to offend the business class, he simply finds more fulfillment in honest wrestling.

Someone who recognizes that Siegfried is far more than a showman is Bertha's brother Theodor. He points out that Siegfried has used his god-given strength to protect the innocent: "In this sense the job of wrestler is majestic. Our friend Siegfried does not just win the public's admiration in the arena when he throws his opponent down. No, he sees his power as a heaven-sent gift which puts him in a position to help hard-pressed people persecuted and abused by powerful miscreants."[2] Siegfried's muscles protect the weak. His altruism contrasts with the egocentric mode of a businessman in capitalism. Since the old system of patriarchy is breaking down, it takes exceptional figures like Siegfried to set things right and reestablish social justice. Like the highwayman in myriad colportage novels, he is the outsider who intervenes when and where it is necessary.

Along with the colportage criticism of modern capitalist rationality, the novel about Germany's superstar wrestler asks why physical strength is not valued as highly as intellectual ability. "Why should physical power not be trained just like the mind and why should it not be viewed as equally important?" asks Siegfried.[3] Through his strength, Siegfried defends old-fashioned chivalry and values like kindness, gentleness, and courtesy. These virtues draw women to the wrestler for his strength and good looks are only the external physiognomic signs of what lies inside him.

Siegfried proves to be society's savior when he intervenes in a tense showdown at the Struve factory in Berlin. His evil foster brother Egon has shown up to foment unrest among the workers. They demand higher wages and will not consider owner Struve's arguments that recent losses make it impossible for him to meet their demands. He also reminds them that a factory owner is not someone who simply exploits workers for profit. They do not understand the risks and burdens, the hard choices that an entrepreneur constantly faces. When the spokesman argues that Struve is a millionaire only because of the workers' labor, he replies that each one of them could be as rich as him if they were prepared to sacrifice for such a goal. Instead, what do they do? "It is a known fact that you beat your wives," claims Struve, "Every Saturday when you receive your wages, you go home drunk and remain intoxicated all of Sunday too."[4] He also lets them know, that he rejected an offer from a company to buy the factory because it would not agree to build a hospital for the workers.

Egon is among the crowd, stoking the flames of anger. The situation gets tense and dangerous. Siegfried appears as a deus ex machina. He picks out Egon and explains to the rebelling workers that this man had also agitated and created chaos in America by inciting racial hatred.[5] But the Americans had an appropriate answer for the firebrand. They tarred and feathered him. The workers turn on Egon demanding that he be lynched.[6] They withdraw their wage demands, realizing that they had been misled and underestimated the good will and benevolence of their boss. He and the foreman shake hands to reestablish social peace. Struve addresses his employees: "See, people, it sometimes happens that children rise up against their father, no matter how well-meaning he is. But what father would not want to give a heartfelt pardon when the children come to ask forgiveness?" Now that order returns, he rewards them all with a modest pay raise. The workers shout, "Three cheers for our kindly factory owner, three cheers for the whole Struve family."[7]

This was the kind of resolution of social tension favored by the melodramatic mode and colportage. Society is one big family and everyone – parents and children – need to accept their roles. Benevolence and obedience result in happiness and prosperity. Confrontation and conflict only bring suffering and destruction. The Struve family celebrate their savior. It remains a mystery why he appeared at the crucial moment, but then one could also ask why he was in San Francisco when the earthquake struck, why he was in Queen Draga's chamber when the assassins arrived. What the colportage reader really wanted was sensation after sensation, not necessarily a story following the parameters of realism or logic – this despite colportage's many subtitles claiming that the stories were taken from real life. In the Weimar Republic, when censors were forced to read novels on account of the 1926 law against trashy literature, they often expressed outrage about colportage's penchant for heaping one impossibility on another. Very few of them showed the least sympathy for a mode of reading that just did not fit their own.

Siegfried's courting of Bertha Struve, the factory owner's daughter, and their marriage is a story filled with melodramatic twists and turns. The great wrestler does not know that his bride-to-be has been deflowered by his counterpart Egon, the devil incarnate. In a dishonest scheme, the factory owner and Bertha want a speedy marriage which might also cover up the fact that Bertha is pregnant. Theodor, Bertha's brother, knows that such a rotten deal can only have disastrous consequences. He warns his father not to betray Siegfried with such deceit, but father Struve wants to ward off all possibility of a scandal and sees a quick marriage as the only way out.

Poor, innocent Siegfried does not realize what he is getting into. He claims, "I know that I am bringing home a woman who will give me the most valuable thing a girl can possess – her virginity!" This illusion is quickly shattered after the marriage when he receives a mysterious letter informing him of the real situation. His first reaction is to beat Bertha, but the thought of beating a woman is repugnant to him. "Betrayed," Siegfried cries out, "shamefully betrayed, and I thought I was joining an honest family where morality rules... and that was not capable of lying."[8]

Overcome by hostile emotions, Siegfried first lays the blame on Bertha. He argues that a man cannot rape a woman unless there is some measure of compliance. This traditional masculinist view later gives way to one more amenable to considering Bertha's protest. She declares that people always unfairly blame the woman. Siegfried knows how evil his foster brother is and acknowledges that "since Egon carried out this terrible crime, so you are less guilty than I first thought."[9] Still, he cannot remain together with Bertha for this would mean living with someone who is disgraced. He confesses to Theodor, "I feel a revulsion against her even if she is as beautiful as Venus. [Egon] is nothing less than a predator."[10] Theodor begs Siegfried not to divorce Bertha as this would bring shame to the family. He promises that the illegitimate child will be born in secrecy and then given to good foster parents. This offer assuages Siegfried's anger. He departs Berlin without filing for divorce.

8. Wilhelmine Women and their Wrestler

The title Das Weib des Ringkämpfers is misleading because Bertha, who will be rehabilitated at novel's end, only appears halfway through the story. Normally, a colportage novel starts with a romance ordained in heaven that, after innumerable challenges and separations, concludes with the apotheosis of marriage. In Büttner's narrative it first seems that Siegfried's foster sister Hilde will be the hero's guiding star from beginning to end. Perhaps on account of her status as a type of sibling, the author felt or was told that developing such a romance smacked of incest. Hilde is removed from the story after the traumatic getaway from the American Indians. Leroy and Siegfried convinced Hilde to play along with the young chief's plan to marry her so that they can, in a surprise move, escape. She is told to stab Eagle Feather and run down to the river where Leroy and Siegfried wait in a canoe.

The escape works but does not go according to plan. Hilde only wounds her new husband and he chases her to the river. There is a brutal fight that ends when Siegfried hits Eagle Feather so hard with a tomahawk that the young American Indian is decapitated. The head falls into Hilde's lap. It is a trauma from which she will never recover. Siegfried and Leroy try their best to help her but she eventually dies in a German insane asylum. So the author eliminates a problematical figure from the narrative and "frees" Siegfried from any long-term commitment. Instead of one hero and one heroine, the main character has multiple relationships with women. Interestingly, it is almost always the women who initiate these romances. A more accurate title would have been Die Weiber des Ringkämpfers (The Wrestler's Women), but such a title may have raised too many eyebrows by suggesting a celebrity wrestler can have as many women as he pleases.

Büttner's presentation of the female characters in WRK oscillates between old stereotyped caricatures of women to more intriguing portrayals of "new women" breaking with nineteenth century standardized roles. Around the year of the novel's publication, 1907, profound transformations were taking place in German society. Sexual behavior and occupational roles were changing. Gabriele Reuter's bestseller Aus guter Familie (1895) had openly discussed female sexuality. In 1905 August Forel published Die sexuelle Frau. The universities of Heidelberg and Freiburg admitted and matriculated women starting in 1900. More and more middle class parents expected improved educational opportunities for their daughters. New jobs like social worker, telephone operator, and typist opened up careers for women. In 1905 Bertha von Suttner received the first Nobel Peace Prize. Along with change came male resistance. Neurologist Paul Julius Möbius published Über den physiologischen Schwachsinn des Weibes (About the Physiological Mental Deficiency of Women) in 1900. This hostile work provoked an instant response from women writers like Hedwig Dohm's Die Antifeministen (1902), Oda Olberg's Das Weib und der Intellektualismus (1902), and Johanna Elberskirchen's Feminismus und Wissenschaft (1903). In 1904 a World Congress of Women met in Berlin. Its participants were invited to the royal palace by Queen Auguste Victoria.

Topics like how women could combine jobs and family work, the concepts of "free love" and pre-marital sex, or how society should improve the treatment of illegitimate children gained public notice. The suffragettes in England and the U.S. sparked great interest in Germany. Against this backdrop, Büttner created his female characters who are not, with one exception, feminists, but do manifest their wishes and desires in ways that would have been unacceptable in an earlier time. As characters they are more interesting and more believable than Siegfried who is as unchanging as a marble statue.

One of Siegfried's first adventures with a female admirer takes place in Scotland, a romantic land where people still believe in "old myths and fairytales."[1] Siegfried is staying in shape by pulling oak trees out of the ground when he hears a shriek. A woman on horseback has been thrown out of her saddle. On the ground she is attacked by a stag with large antlers. Siegfried intervenes. Holding the wild animal down, he tells the woman to finish the beast off with her lance. "Such a beautiful woman he had never seen before," thought Siegfried, "He had seldom seen such a tall, physically strong figure... and had noticed immediately she possessed enormous strength."[2] Her presence evokes a mythical past: "The way she stood there leaning on her spear... she looked like one of those Valkyries that in ancient times may have hunted here."[3] Lady Maria Stratford invites her rescuer to visit her castle. When Siegfried introduces himself, she says she has read all about him in the newspapers.

Maria tells Siegfried she would like to test her strength against his. So far no man has been able to defeat her. Siegfried replies hesitantly that he has never wrestled a woman and cannot imagine doing so. This kind of role reversal tantalized turn-of-the-century society and raised all sorts of questions about gender roles. It should not, however, be viewed as part of a conscious attempt by the colportage writer to present an emancipated female figure. Instead it actually played more into turn-of-the-century prejudices and characterizations of dangerous female sexuality and the predatory nature of "the woman vampire." Still, a female reader could interpret the episode as illustrating alternate female behavior.

Maria reveals herself to have an insatiable appetite for men. She uses them and, when she has had enough, she tosses them over the castle's tower. Despite the monstrous caricature, her behavior may have tickled the fancy of female readers. When she initiates physical contact with Siegfried by giving him a long kiss, he asks if she has forgotten her husband. "I belong to myself!" she answers proudly, "There is no one in the world who can give me an order, nor is there anyone who has the right to forbid me from anything!"[4]

Picture 11: Dora Helms was born around 1890 in Berlin. In 1907 she was displayed in Berlin's Passage Panoptikum. She wears the attire of the goddess Germania. Oversized or physically powerful women were staple features at Wilhelmine fairgrounds.

Andenken an Brunhilde, die Deutsche Riesin, 18 Jahre alt.

This fierce independence does not mean that Maria has eliminated all traditional gender norms. She tells Siegfried that in him she has finally found someone "truly worthy of being called a man." In contrast, all other men are "weaklings, female beings [weibische Naturen]."[5] Siegfried encounters a pale young man in the castle who tells him he is one of Maria's many victims. He warns Siegfried that she is a vampire who sucks blood out of men.[6] Siegfried finds it all unbelievable, but the stranger refers to historical figures like the ancient Roman Messalina who "loved men to death."[7]

Picture 12: Across the border in France, a less nationalistic strong woman shows off her weight-lifting abilities to a crowd of school boys. She is obviously the star of the show (Postcard 1911).

In the meantime Leroy wonders where Siegfried is and inquires about the mysterious castle. He is told about beautiful, dangerous Maria. One man compares her to the legendary Brunhilde of the Nibelungen myth who was bestowed with abnormal strength and briefly

subjugated Siegfried, the legend's hero.[8] Siegfried the Wrestler refuses
to be outdone by his namesake. When Maria realizes that Siegfried will
not submit to her wishes she tries to throw him from the tower. The
skilled wrestler defies her and slowly lifts her before he drops her deep
down into the chasm. He tells Leroy that this wrestling match meant life
or death. The local population congratulates Siegfried and thanks him
for having freed the area from the woman stricken with "love madness"
and the killer of many male victims.

The Maria episode reveals the sort of ambiguous position women oc-
cupy in WRK. On the one hand, the novel portrays role reversals that certainly let readers reflect on possibilities for women who did not conform
to traditional gender roles. Even Maria's killing of a dozen men contradicts the usual figure of the male serial killer with his multiple female
victims. Yet her powerful individualism betrays a weakness that turn-
of-the-century culture reserved for women: madness.

In WRK several women go insane. One is Siegfried's mother. She
lost her sanity when Siegfried was taken from her on account of the in-
correct prediction that he would soon perish. In a story-within-a-story,
we learn of Leroy's tragic romance with the incurably insane Diana. The
heroine Hilde, Siegfried's foster sister and first love, degenerates into
insanity when confronted with the terrible decapitation of her American Indian suitor. These cases all reflect the belief that women were far
more prone to mental illness because they lacked man's rational capaci-
ties and were overcharged with emotions and primitive instincts. Here
too the colportage novel mirrored and reflected ideas and imagery typical of turn-of-the-century culture.

The conflict about new roles for women is revealed when a father
complains to Siegfried that his daughter Aveline is determined to de-
velop her physical strength and engage in sports. The father says that this
is an aberration for a sixteen-year-old girl. She enjoys fencing, horseback riding, swimming, and soccer. Now, of all things, she wants to take
up wrestling![9] The father tells how she was inspired seeing pictures of
Siegfried in French illustrated journals and that she claims to love him.
Siegfried reassures the distraught father that it is a passing infatuation.
He points out that the girl is not in love with him, but with his picture.

Pictures 13: and 14: Along with the Riesendame (giant lady), women wrestling matches were popular sideshows. A Dresden woman wrestler attracts attention by flexing her muscles (Postcard 1903). The Schweighofer wrestling team traveled about in 1903 demonstrating their skills (Postcard 1913).

A more serious love develops between Siegfried and an Italian woman during a vacation that Leroy has arranged. Siegfried needs a break after numerous victorious matches and before he faces George Hackenschmidt, the best wrestler in the world. Leroy warns that Rome could be a place of danger for Siegfried: "Nowhere are people more passionate, nowhere are people more poorly behaved than in Italy. Avoid any altercation because they are quick to pull out the stiletto. Even more than the stiletto, watch out for the dark eyes of the ladies."[10] Such warnings let the reader know that Siegfried is about to have a romantic adventure in Italy.

The Roman Carnival is in full swing but Siegfried shows little interest because he receives news from Germany that Hilde is not doing well. He takes a gondola down the Tiber to the Mediterranean Sea so he can enjoy a lovely view of the Sabine Hills and the Eternal City. In these scenes, Büttner reveals his lack of geographical knowledge. Rome is not visible from the Mediterranean, nor were there any Venetian gondolas on the Tiber River! Despite Siegfried's indifferent mood, the carnival begins to interest him when he hears that Rome's most beautiful woman presides over the parade as carnival queen. When the dark-haired beauty passes by, she and Siegfried exchange meaningful glances. Later, at a festivity, she picks Siegfried as her consort instead of her fiancée.

Another example of a self-determined woman, carnival queen Violetta spirits Siegfried away from the festivities and takes him to an empty villa on the Roman outskirts. She tells Siegfried she can only have a short affair because she will be marrying her fiancée in a week. Violetta also confides that she does not expect much from marriage. She will have children and family worries, sooner or later her husband will beat her. Then she will no longer love her husband for a woman cannot love a man who has beaten her.[11] Siegfried is consternated. Violetta goes into the garden to get water from a well. He hears a scream and finds Violetta stabbed to death. Siegfried figures the jilted fiancée took revenge, but later it becomes clear that she was murdered by someone else by mistake.

From this dangerous liaison, Siegfried moves on to another with Elena, the Marquise of Rivoli. In a convoluted, complicated plot she is kidnapped by highwayman Riccardo Diavolo. Siegfried infiltrates the bandits and helps her escape. She falls in love with her rescuer and refuses to return to her husband. Elena affirms: "We live in a century in which personal freedom of every individual is guaranteed. I hardly believe any court of law would force a woman to return to a man she does not love, who fills her with disgust."[12] When Leroy finds out about this new romance, he expresses his disappointment in his charge: "…Here in this land of jealousy with its fatal consequences, you started an affair with a married woman?"[13]

Towards the novel's end, Leroy and Siegfried enjoy the charms and amusements of Vienna as they await the match with the world-famous George Hackenschmidt. They are having dinner at the Prater's Eisvogel Restaurant. A womens' orchestra is playing Viennese songs "so light, so sparkling… it goes into the blood."[14] The pretty conductor catches Siegfried's eye. Outside the establishment, Siegfried happens to cross paths with Franzi, the band's leader. She gives him a rose. They talk and Franzi impresses him with her knowledge about the mythological Siegfried in the Nibelungen myth. Once more inside, she tells her assistant to strike up the band. She turns to Siegfried and says, "…do you hear the waltz, beautiful wrestler? Oh, with you I could fly away forever in a waltz…"[15] The couple dances to the lovely melody.

Picture 15: Colportage author Heinrich Büttner liked to use real locations to increase the authenticity of his stories. One such place was the famous Eisvogel Restaurant in Vienna's Prater amusement park (Postcard 1915).

A dark cloud descends over Franzi when a gentleman appears at the end of the concert. It is Egon. He holds power over Franzi because he knows that her father is a counterfeiter wanted by the police. Egon orders Franzi to arrange a rendezvous with Siegfried at a specific Viennese address. She reluctantly acquiesces. Egon locks the couple in and sets the house on fire hoping to kill them both. The firemen and a doctor manage to revive Siegfried, but the not so fortunate Franzi has expired.

Picture 16: Vienna's women orchestras were popular in Austria and Germany. This postcard (stamped in 1913) of the Louise Rosenkranz Orchestra was purchased at the Welt-Restaurant Societé, Dresden, a large venue for variety shows.

Vienna has also drawn Bertha, Siegfried's abandoned wife, back into the picture. She wants to avenge herself on Egon who left her defiled and pregnant in Berlin. She is armed with a revolver and a bottle of poison. Egon finds out about her plans and captures her. Leroy and Siegfried figure out where he holds Bertha prisoner. They call the police and free her. In the basement of a large restaurant they find the counterfeiters and the ringleader. Egon is arrested for counterfeiting, robbery, and murder. He stabs himself. Before dying, he asks for forgiveness. He admits to drugging and raping Bertha so her "guilt" is proven wrong. Siegfried embraces Bertha, declaring her "morally pure."[16] Egon admits that wasting the family fortune of the von Rüden estate did not bring him happiness. He has only brought shame to the family. Egon also manages to give Siegfried the documents that prove he is the real heir to the noble family's name and fortune. As in practically all colportage novels, such an ending reintegrates a lost noble title with an appropriately noble char-

acter and thus puts the paternal world back in order. What had originally upset the order was Count von Rüden's horrifyingly unnatural decision to abandon his own sickly baby Siegfried and to replace him with
the healthy stranger Egon. Such a selfish, irresponsible act distresses the
universal system and calls for retribution. Siegfried's evolution to a kind
of superman also signals a divine intervention to set things straight.

Siegfried wins another wrestling championship in Berlin, but what
makes him most happy is his restored marriage with Bertha: "He hon-
estly won the title of world champion. What made him a thousand times
happier than being crowned king of the wrestlers, was his love for Bertha
and her love for him."[17] As interesting as the character Bertha may be,
she does not really meet the standard qualification for a colportage heroine. She simply does not appear often enough in the narrative to serve
as the female pendant to Siegfried. Of course, Siegfried could not have
his countless other adventures with women if he also had a true partner
throughout. This abnormal quality to WRK could have made it more or
less appealing to the reader, depending on their expectations. Those who
wanted good old-fashioned formulaic colportage would have been disappointed. Those who wanted something different from the norm may
have found it more interesting.

Unlike Bertha, the character Karla appears over and over again in the
novel from start to finish. She is unusual in that she does not fit the flat,
unchanging portrayal typical of most colportage characters. She is introduced as the pretty step-daughter of a decadent Polish countess who literally wants to sell her to the Turkish wrestler Kara Achmed. The mother
suffers from the common aristocratic illness of compulsive gambling.
Siegfried finds out about her and asks in shock: "What kind of mother
sells her child?" The reader's sympathies for Karla diminish when he or
she learns that Karla flirts with Egon and is his partner in crime. The
levels of evil that she and Egon are willing to reach are astonishing. In
order to acquire Egon's inheritance as soon as possible they plan to poison his adoptive father Count von Rüden. The old man has recently hired
Siegfried as a servant, not realizing that he is his firstborn son, given
away at birth to the blacksmith Sebastian Trutz. In the count's house,
Siegfried chances to see Karla spraying "perfume" in the bedroom. It is a

poison. Egon appears and decides to choke his father to death. Siegfried intervenes. The count wakes up, realizing that Egon had tried to kill him. He disowns his adopted son and tells the story of why he exchanged his biological son for the substituted baby Egon. The old man asks for and receives forgiveness from Siegfried for his heinous crime (that stabbed at the heart of patriarchy). Egon and Karla are banished. The count calls Karla a snake and Egon a bastard. He tries to change his testament, but overcome with emotion, he dies before being able to do so. The notary regretfully tells Siegfried that Egon remains the legal heir to the von Rüden fortune.

Karla, betrayed by Egon, starts an affair with the lion-tamer Batty.[18] They plan to have a lion kill Egon during a performance. The plan would have worked but Siegfried comes to the rescue of his worthless foster brother. Siegfried jumps on the lion's back and then shoots him in the head.[19] The startled crowd applauds Siegfried's courage, while Karla and Batty escape. Three hundred pages later, the reader finds Karla has contracted yellow fever in Louisiana and Batty cruelly abandons her to her fate. Egon replaces Batty as he restarts his relationship to the stricken, but recovering Karla. The couple do not see eye to eye on Siegfried: his burning desire is to gain revenge, but this obsession leaves her cold.[20]

Eight hundred pages later we see an improved version of Karla. She and Siegfried end up on a desert island after they have been forcibly disembarked from a mutinying ship (they had refused to join the mutineers). Siegfried still detests her, but he has to admit that Karla shows courage and resilience on the lonely island. Karla knows how to catch fish and collect oysters. While Siegfried looks out for possible rescue ships, Karla likes their solitude on the island and hopes that one day he will warm up to her and forgive her past sins. Karla even nurses him back to health after he catches malaria. She openly declares her love for the wrestler. In secret, she puts out the fires that he starts every night in an attempt to get a passing ship's attention. Just as Siegfried seems like he is going to embrace a solitary life with Karla, a ship arrives to save them both.

More than one thousand pages on, Karla appears in her final role. She has become an experienced detective and managed to gain respect even from her male colleagues. Vienna's police chief is first skeptical but then acknowledges her abilities: "There was so much beauty, power, energy, and nobility in her demeanor," that the police president said, "this lady can definitely accomplish more than a male detective!"[21] In Vienna her first assignment is difficult. She is supposed to trail and protect Siegfried from an attack by a suspicious confidence man [Egon]. The mission evokes barely slumbering feelings in her. When Egon tries to recruit her, she resists. Her new, good side prevails as she helps Bertha escape from a band of criminals. At novel's end, Karla, once the victim of her gambling-crazed mother, is a top police officer on her way to New York where she will become the most famous woman detective in the United States.

While women characters in WRK are described with all sorts of turn-of-the-century prejudices and clichés, it is also obvious that these women are no wallflowers. They are headstrong and unyielding in realizing their ambitions and plans. They do not give in to male wishes, nor do they accept unfair double standards. As such, they could have been role models for some female readers who also wished to realize aims and desires opposed by a male-dominated culture and society. Bertha wants to marry a wrestler against the will of her wealthy father. Aveline is determined to try out all sorts of sports formerly reserved for men. Livia risks her life in the interest of revolution. Karla succeeds in a career where few women have gone before. Violetta and Elena do not allow jealous men to block their private aims and goals.

9. The Contradictions of Colportage: Paternalism and Populism

One wonders how a novel pledging allegiance to seemingly outworn patriarchal and paternalist notions could include such contradicting, pro-female accents. Yet colportage literature was the perfect place to draw in and fuse multiple and contrary currents of social thought, cultural prejudice, and foggy political ideas. The books were written in a hurry with little or no thought given to ideological coherence. The main point was to entertain not to lecture, to amuse, not to spread doctrines. These often denigrated works of literature open up an intriguing glimpse into notions and thoughts that floated freely and unselfconsciously about in the turn-of-the-century popular mind. Colportage novels thus document a significant viewpoint not preserved in most other cultural artifacts. For a full version of the Zeitgeist, this view needs to be included.

Here and there, Büttner made cutting, condescending remarks about working class women. This is puzzling when one considers that these women were a major target group of readers for every colportage novel. When Leroy meets Diana he distinguishes her from proletarian lowlife: "I observed such good manners that she could not possibly belong to the working class. This was neither a factory girl...nor a servant girl. This must be a girl coming from a good family."[1] When a Russian noblewoman falls in love with a brutish Cossack wrestler, Büttner comments, "...he possessed everything that usually only factory girls admired or that servant girls raved about."[2]

Was this oblique criticism simply the author's own prejudice or was he attempting to modify lower class behavior by attacking it? Did colportage authors aspire to popularity among the lower classes while, at the same time, maintaining that society's higher virtues were embodied in the middle classes?

Colportage writers had a critical view of human behavior, especially when it was no longer framed in a stabilized, organic family setting. What was going wrong in modern society was that people were no longer accepting or fulfilling their assigned natural roles. Worst of all were the many corrupt exponents of the aristocracy. Instead of being role models, they were often gamblers, lechers, people with no moral compass. Bertha's father, the capitalist factory owner Struve, behaves mostly according to the benign mores of an enlightened, caring captain of industry. His attempt to deceive Siegfried in the marriage of his daughter Bertha reveals that he too could put self-interest ahead of trust and honesty. For his workers, though, he provides secure jobs, health care, and a pension plan.[3] When they demand higher wages, he views them as ingrates and wonders why they extol class solidarity instead of showing him the loyalty he deserves. A bitter struggle is averted only because Siegfried restores social peace after revealing how Egon has misled the workers and artificially incited class hostility.

The highwayman as savior of the lower class was another theme often central to colportage novels. This is not the case in WRK because Siegfried the Wrestler has replaced the old-fashioned renegade bandit-savior. Yet Büttner could not resist incorporating a lengthy highwayman episode about the Italian brigand Riccardo Diavolo into his narrative. The latter is viewed by the lower class population as their protector and one who can cancel out many of society's injustices against the poor. This does not mean that all criminals are anti-heroes in WRK. It depends on the context. Italian brigands follow a popular rural tradition that set up an alternative form of patriarchy. Lower class thieves in the city have no redeeming qualities. The episode featuring the criminal girl Fanchon and the gang called "the Apaches of Paris," a plagiarized narrative copy of Eugène Sue's The Mysteries of Paris, shows only destitution and self-destruction. The workers and their political allies were misled by leftist firebrands, like the Russian nihilist Livia, who wanted to solve society's problems through a violent overthrow of the tsar. Such a goal conflicted with the melodramatic mode of colportage. Revolution was not needed, but the restoration of a kind-hearted, benevolent patriarchy would resolve contemporary problems. Only this system of obligation from above and deference from below could bring social peace. Outside the ideals of family unity and divinely-inspired monarchy, reigned a world out of control that inevitably unleashed the beast in man.

Since colportage novels often admitted that monarchs were not up to task and nobility was largely corrupt and immoral, the proposed ideology could hardly provide a clear political guideline. In fact, the populist contradictions within the colportage worldview were revealed in subjects like the legal system and the execution of justice. Colportage rejects the state's laws. These are too easily manipulated to serve the rich and powerful, and often misused to oppress the poor. Siegfried is tried twice in WRK and both times narrowly escapes from an unjust death sentence. Illustrations of courts in the book show grim, cold-hearted bureaucrats presiding and carrying out a corrupted form of justice.

In the Wild West, Siegfried and Leroy witness a kind of popular justice they are unfamiliar with. An angry crowd wants to lynch the notorious bandit "Black Bob." They are opposed by an army lieutenant who warns them about taking the law into their own hands. Siegfried wants to assist the officer when it appears that the crowd may push him aside, but Leroy tells Siegfried not to interfere. He explains that juries in the West can easily be bribed or intimidated. There is more justice in a lynch mob. The mob shouts, "We don't trust the judges! The people's voice is God's voice! [Volkesstimme ist Gottesstimme!]" This claim to represent heavenly-sent retribution hardly seems compatible with what ensues. A kangaroo court presided by an aged, grey-bearded man, condemns the criminal to death. Since Bob has even killed women and children, popular justice calls for an appropriately brutal death. He is tied between two wild horses pulling in opposite directions: "[The cowboys] worked with spurs and whips and then – a scream rang out over the crowd, a cheer of jubilation accompanied the catastrophe. Black Bob's body was ripped into pieces, his blood flowed into the dust of the street, and the stallions galloped away in different directions. Tied to one horse's tail were the criminal's upper body and head. The other dragged away the abdomen and legs."[4] This kind of excessive bloodshed punctuated the narrative at various points and likely appealed to a sizable portion of colportage readers who could not find such shocking violence in other literature. Wilhelmine press laws tolerated it, while the later, post-1926 censorship of the Weimar Republic would not.

Colportage could not hide its support for "popular justice." Lynch mobs were expressions of the people's will and a justice not mediated by formalities that led to verdicts making little sense to laymen. How could writers trust mob rule when, in other circumstances, the mob is presented as mean and destructive, as a danger to all? Such contradictions must have confused the reader and weakened a sort of ideology that claimed to bring people together under the auspices of family paternalism. Could lynch justice and patriarchy be made compatible? Colportage writers seem to have felt that both were somehow rudimentarily "organic," derived from nature, and thus superior to government laws based on rational, enlightenment values and the artificial constructs of modern society.

Legal unfairness was one thing, the unfair distribution of wealth another. Nowhere could the wheel of fortune turn more drastically than at the casino of Monte Carlo. This mecca of gambling fascinated everyone because one could enter its halls as a pauper and leave as a millionaire, or vice versa. For colportage, with its love of extremes, it was an ideal stage for an installment episode. Leroy and Siegfried want to recover from their Italian adventures in the little seaside principality located between Italy and France. When Siegfried first sees the place he exclaims, "It is paradise on earth!"[5] The mild climate promotes the growth of palm trees and roses that can be found in "the wonderful gardens." Gorgeous hotels provide visitors with the same amenities they would find in Paris. What stands out above everything, however, is the great white casino building, a temple to money. Inside gold abounds, the purple carpets soften the gamblers' steps, and the walls are artistically decorated: "The gambling idol is paid homage in this marble palace."[6] Everyone wants to try their luck.

Father-figure Leroy warns Siegfried of the risks of gambling and tells him just to be an observer. Siegfried watches the winning and losing happening at the roulette table. He cannot resist the temptation to try his luck. He quickly loses seven hundred francs and recognizes that Leroy was right. His mentor tells him that "for people who work, who have to achieve something for their income... the games of Monte Carlo are unsuitable."[7] Before leaving the casino, Leroy reminds Siegfried that they are lodged at the Hotel de Mediterranée, room number thirteen. He comments that a gambler would never stay in a room with a jinxed number. Siegfried, however, likes the number. He was born on the thirteenth, he won his first wrestling match on the thirteenth, and he considers it a lucky number. This discussion, the reader understands, is a portent for some major event or drama. Colportage thrived on fateful prognostications that stimulated the superstitious imaginary. This was another reason why educated critics found colportage to be downright dangerous and why its supposedly lower class readers found it compelling. It gave form to their own alternative culture.

Later on Siegfried leaves the casino. In a quiet park, he is grabbed from behind, a bag is placed over his head, and several men carry him to a ship named "the Savior." The next morning Siegfried is introduced to Captain Grigoleitis. A former gambler, the eccentric character has vowed to battle the gambling sickness emanating from Monte Carlo. He tells Siegfried that every year he abducts three people whom he has identified as stricken by gambling fever in order to save them and bring them to his anti-gambling utopian island. Siegfried wants no part of it and defies Grigoleitis, warning that he will use the first opportunity to escape.

The Mediterranean island proves to be of great beauty, its inhabitants seem blissfully content. For a while Siegfried is puzzled by the place and its strange, seemingly benevolent tyrant who lives in a sumptuous palace. Siegfried soon learns that the utopian island with its lovely white-washed houses basking in the sun, is nothing but a facade. A young woman named Elektra tells him the island's wealth is based on piracy. Siegfried and Elektra undertake a dangerous attempt to escape. After a major mishap, they luckily witness the demise of the island dictator in a sea battle with a Greek warship.

The episode combines exotic and utopian/dystopian elements with the excitement of the hero's escape adventure in the company of an attractive young victim of turn-of-the-century human trafficking or what was called white slavery (another popular theme for colportage).[8] Seemingly a benign apostle of anti-gambling, Grigoleitis is revealed as a false prophet and nothing more than a pirate. It is Siegfried who fulfills the role of paternalist defender as he returns the eighteen year-old Elektra to her grateful Greek family. Büttner did not choose the name Elektra accidently. In Homeric mythology she is the classic avenger of a patricide.

The comforting aspect of the novel is that no matter how dire the straits, the reader knows that Siegfried will emerge triumphant. Siegfried is the turn-of-the-century link between invincible mythological gods and the twentieth century superhero. What makes him distinct and closely tied to the nineteenth century is the melodramatic mode in which he operates. In contrast to his evil counterpart Egon, who at one point wants to commit patricide (Siegfried calls him Vatermörder), Siegfried always seeks to preserve the social hierarchy. Whether it is convincing angry factory workers in Berlin to appreciate their benevolent boss, or returning a kidnapped daughter to her family in Greece, Siegfried wants social and family harmony. Egon is the evil factor who thrives on crime, conflict, and social dissolution. He is "a devil in human form" and has a global record of trouble-making, always appearing to challenge his noble opposite.[9] He uses his good looks and charms to take advantage of women and satisfy his lust. Never can he offer the honest, spontaneous, selfless love that characterizes Siegfried. He meets justice in the form of a lynch mob in New Orleans that instead of hanging him decides in favor of tarring and feathering. Egon had plotted to have Siegfried injected with yellow fever by a black wrestler during a match. The plot fails but the match sparks racial street battles after incitement by Egon. He claims the wrestling match was rigged. Like the lynch mob that condemned "Black Bob" to death, this violent form of justice is construed as legitimate because it is sanctioned by authentic popular will.

Leroy explains that, "the people here are rawer and more brutal... than Europeans, but their passions and cravings transform themselves unveiled and do not bow down to written law and custom. Instead they do what nature demands of them."[10] Populism and patriarchy achieve a fragile synthesis: at their source, they both express the unalterable exigencies of nature, whether in the form of a raw, popular sensibility for justice or in the longing for family harmony with its poles of paternal responsibility and subordinate deference. If this was all too complicated for the average reader to understand, there was Siegfried's reassuring claim that "my Kaiser will not permit injustice being done to any of his subjects."[11]

Siegfried's extraordinary powers and fighting skills occasionally are lethal. Sometimes he regrets killing, as when he smashes an Italian bandit's skull with a rifle butt.[12] On the other hand, if lethal force is necessary, Siegfried has no qualms. "Do I not possess powers that allow me to prevail over everyone?" he asks as he takes on the dangerous Apaches of Paris. This gift of invincible power has higher, occult origins. He concludes: "So, I can kill if it is necessary."[13]

He proceeds to destroy the most dangerous Parisian gang. The Paris police chief thanks him and offers him a job. Siegfried replies he is not suited and wants to return to wrestling. His help for the police came naturally and should simply be interpreted as a citizen's duty: "Bourgeois society [die bürgerliche Gesellschaft] has the duty to defend itself against such beasts as the Apaches…"[14]

For all his travails, Siegfried is rewarded at the novel's end. Bertha's father provides the young couple with "an attractive villa."[15] Siegfried has now been recognized as a genuine nobleman carrying the title of Count von Rüden. Nobility and strength are united with material wealth and bourgeois patrimony. The reader does not get the impression that the hero surrenders to stasis, for as long as he gives evidence of his virtuoso abilities, new laurels are laid at his feet.[16]

10. Postscript: Heinrich Büttner's First Colportage Novel of 1892

Heinrich Büttner's first colportage novel Ferdinand Lassalle der Held des Volkes oder um Liebe getötet (Ferdinand Lassalle the People's Hero or Killed for Love) was published in 1892–1893. Like WRK, the subject matter was highly original. Certainly the dramatic life of one of the founders of social democracy was perfect material for a serial novel. In particular, his tragic death at age thirty-nine in a duel over a woman and a romance gone bad could generate interest among a readership hungry for scandal and melodrama. In typical colportage manner, the subtitle claimed veracity by means of careful research by the author of letters, documents, and statements made by Lassalle's relatives. Nothing could be further from the truth. Much of the novel consisted of side narratives that had little or nothing to do with Ferdinand Lassalle at all. Thus Büttner devoted a lengthy episode to a stingy Jewish moneylender named Nathan Lewysohn and his beautiful, altruistic daughter Rosa.

In stark contrast to the comments made in WRK where Büttner emphasized that Jewish moneylenders were no worse than their Christian counterparts, in Ferdinand Lassalle he creates Jewish characters who fit all the negative antisemitic clichés and stereotypes of the times. The 1880s and 1890s were a period of feverish antisemitism. This hateful mood is embodied in the novel. In a key scene, during the Revolution of 1848, a crowd storms the elegant city home of Nathan Lewysohn. The angry populace calls out: "Kill the usurer. He has enriched himself through the sweat of the poor. He has stolen millions. Take his money and burn his house down!"[1] The crowd sees its action as a case of revolutionary justice. The scene foreshadows similar ones in WRK (minus the antisemitism), where an aroused vox populi expresses an authentic form of immediate justice truer than that pursued by dry and dusty court tribunals.

Thus the raging destruction and vengeance of a vandalizing, antisemitic mob seems to find approval in this colportage version of revolution: "The populace released its anger on the objects in the house. One struck down pictures and smashed statues. The most expensive items were destroyed. One felt one had the right to ruin the property of a man who had systematically plundered the people."[2] Frightened to death, the moneylender and his Jewish assistants chant Hebrew prayers much to the chagrin of Rosa, who views all this as palpable cowardice. She, instead, holds a knife and is ready to fight. Rosa asks her father if the crowd's accusations are true. He admits his exploitative ways just before the royal army arrives to drive back the mad "revolutionaries." Rosa wants to have nothing more to do with her father. She chooses a new road to humility and purification by joining the proletariat as a factory worker.[3]

The novel portrays Ferdinand Lassalle, leader of the workers, as the opposite of the Jewish moneylenders. While they selfishly live off the people, he devotes his life to them. Turning her back on Nathan Lewysohn, Rosa finds "a shining light" in Ferdinand Lassalle. "Aren't there also noble Jews," she asks, "Oh yes, her eyes lit up with holy fire..." "Ferdinand Lassalle," she said with commotion, "Does he not belong to our race [Stamm]? Isn't he one of the most noble? Don't millions honor him and look up to him? Oh great, noble man! Perhaps only a few of my race are like you, yet through them the curse of misjudgment would be overcome!"[4]

This is how the colportage author links the story of Rosa and the Jewish moneylenders with the story of Ferdinand Lassalle, the workers' Jewish hero. Hatred and love, cowardly Jews and heroic Jews, make for splendid melodrama. To what extent the story succeeded in attracting a readership is hard to say, but we do at least know that it met with disapproval in the official SPD press and among its readers. Several readers expressed anger in letters to the editor of Vorwärts. One reader warned that the colportage novel <u>Ferdinand Lassalle</u> was a fraudulent piece of literary junk [<u>ein Schwindelmachwerk</u>]. "Show whomever offers you this trash to the door," advised the anonymous reader.[5] A week later, another reader expressed outrage that the installment novel was being sold by a bookstore that claimed affiliation with social democracy. He suggested that working class customers respond appropriately to such "a swindle entrepreneur" by boycotting him.[6]

Finally, we need to ask who was Heinrich Büttner? No biographical data exists. It seems most likely that Büttner is one of many pseudonyms used by the prolific Jewish colportage writer Heinrich Sochaczewsky (1861–1922). He wrote more than thirty potboilers between 1890 and 1914. His favorite pseudonym was Victor von Falk. Besides his gigantic output of novels, little is known about Sochaczewsky. He is also the likely author of <u>Königin Draga, das Verhängnis von Serbien</u> (1903–1904).

Part Two

The Illustrations

Turn-of-the-century subscribers to colportage novels expected a full-page illustration at the beginning of each installment. The quality of these pictures ranged from mediocre, even primitive, all the way up to very good and artistically original. In her study of German colportage, Jessica Plummer discusses how illustrations helped gain customers for this literary genre.

> Coupling standalone serial literature with illustrations was an important innovation, and the illustrations included with each part is a recognizable format that colportage novels took for themselves. The reproduction of illustrations, in general, was growing cheaper thanks to new technologies, and it was increasingly coming into vogue as a way to sell all kinds of texts, especially to sell them to buyers outside of the clientele of the traditional bookseller. The combination of illustrations and short texts were especially important for the reception of the stories among less educated and lower class readers.[1]

The following description and analysis of WRK illustrations seeks to reveal how they contributed to the story's presentation, accentuating particular topics that the publishers and illustrators thought appealing for their customers and readers. At times it appears that considerable effort was placed in producing a picture that would enhance the story and whet the reader's appetite for more. At other times, the pictures are either dull or barely relevant and appear to be mechanically made and placed according to a pre-established format. Sometimes mistakes were made and pictures were utilized that did not conform to the text. WRK's more compelling illustrations have been selected for this study. For comparative purposes, a few illustrations have been included from Büttner's colportage novels, <u>Ferdinand Lassalle</u> (1892–1893) and <u>Wanda, die Geliebte des Fremdenlegionärs</u> (1914).

1A. Siegfried as Rescuer

Illustration [1-Frontispiece] is dense with symbolism. Like the legendary Siegfried of the Nibelungen, this Siegfried has forged his own weaponry and uses it to vanquish his adversary. The English boxer and kidnapper Bob Craven pulls Hilde by her hair, unaware that he is about to be slain by Hilde's outraged foster brother. "Remove your filthy hands from her or you are dead," calls Siegfried. He frees Hilde from a terrible fate while protecting the family honor and eliminating the sadistic English villain.

In the second illustration [2–24], the colportage artist shows Siegfried fighting Kara Achmed, the famed Turkish wrestler. He has already defeated him in a wrestling match but now rescues Karla, the step-daughter of a Polish countess, from a fate similar to that planned for Hilde. Kara Achmed's strained facial features reveal a not quite human face with bulging, bug-like eyes. The falling fez symbolizes the Turk's defeat at the hands of the European.

1A. Siegfried as Rescuer

1-Frontispiece   2-24

1B.

1B.

27-624   54-1272

Illustration [27–624] shows Siegfried holding Hilde and swimming to shore after they escape a prairie fire and a herd of stampeding buffalos.

In Illustration [54–1272] Siegfried carries Elena, an Italian noblewoman who had been kidnapped by a criminal gang, back to her Monte Carlo hotel.

2.   Siegfried the Wrestler

Büttner and the novel's illustrator wanted to show how wrestling appealed not only to the common people in Illustration [80–1896]. Here the tsar and tsarina view their own star wrestler and the German challenger shortly before the latter's victory.

Siegfried's only defeat is depicted in Illustration [65–1536] where a gender reversal has taken place. Siegfried's inborn chivalry does not permit him to throw a woman so he gives in to her instead and allows himself to be pinned. He explains to his manager that Lord Rudyard Rochester in reality is Lady Naomi Rochester. One look at the picture reveals that indeed the victorious wrestler is a woman. Female wrestlers were a piquant feature of popular culture. The idea or image of a female wrestler defeating a man must have appealed to colportage's large female audience.

2. Siegfried the Wrestler

80-1896   65-1536

3A. Active Women

In WRK it is usually women who start flirtations with Siegfried. They are the main movers of the romances and amorous adventures of the novel's hero. Illustrations [12–264] and [13–288] show scenes from Siegfried's encounter with Lady Maria Stratford, owner of a secluded Scottish castle.

This powerful female vampire consumes men like toys and disposes of them by throwing them off a tower. A local inhabitant tells Siegfried that Maria reminds him of the supernaturally strong Brunhilde who conquered Siegfried of the Nibelungen saga (WRK, p.283). Siegfried and Maria have an argument and she tries to get rid of him in the usual way. Instead, he throws her from the tower. This violent denouement reestablishes traditional gender hierarchy and avenges Maria's many male victims.[2] Siegfried emphasizes the pressure he faced in this battle: "This was my most dangerous wrestling exam! It was a matter of life and death!" (WRK, p.297) Unfortunately, the illustrations fail to show the explosive tension in this rapport.

3A. Active Women

12-264   13-288

3B.

Violetta, Rome's carnival queen, beckons Siegfried to enter a villa on the city outskirts in Illustration [40–936]. Failing to heed his manager Leroy's warnings about Italy, Siegfried goes along and finds himself in a dangerous liaison of love and death. Another Italian intrigue is beautifully pictured in Illustration [45–1056] when Siegfried, dressed as a bandit, rescues the imprisoned Marquise Elena from the feared highwayman, Riccardo Diavolo. Even in a precarious moment of escape, Elena cannot resist kissing Siegfried as she leads the way up a rope ladder.

3B.

40-936   45-1056

3C.

Unusually, in Illustration [88–2088], Siegfried initiates this embrace by bending over the sleeping woman who immediately throws her arms around him. Illustration [93–2208] does a nice job of capturing the ambiance of a café. The pretty widow and Siegfried look at each other. Manager Leroy seems to be thinking, "Oh no! Here we go again!"

3C.

88-2088   93-2208

4A. Romantic Melodrama

Franzi, leader of a Viennese Womens' Orchestra, would like to flee an imploring Egon in Illustration [90–2136]. She cannot just run away because he knows that her father is a counterfeiter wanted by the police. A champagne bottle in ice signals Egon's plan for the evening. Franzi's childlike face contrasts with her womanly body, signaling innocence as well as carnal knowledge – an ambiguity appreciated by colportage readers who relished such contrasts.

In Illustration [98–2328] Karla extends her right arm to prevent Egon's approach. Again a champagne bottle makes his intentions clear, but Karla has learned not to trust falsehearted Egon. He reacts with surprise. The more rounded, fluffy style of this illustration indicates a different artist than the creator of the previous drawing. Publishers sometimes did not bother to coordinate illustrations. In these two pictures, Egon has different facial and body lineaments. The hairstyles are also dissimilar.

4B.

In Illustration [24–552] Karla, at first, resists the lion tamer Batty's advances. In her words, he is just another typical "horribly brash" man. But she then devises a plan whereby the despised Egon will be killed by one of Batty's lions. As someone capable of taming lions, Batty does have a special charming effect on the opposite sex: "Women admire raw strength and most of all, they admire the power that a man can demonstrate over others or even over wild animals…" (WRK, p.554) In Illustration [25–576] Karla plays the coquette as she wraps up the enamored Batty in her diabolical plan to eliminate Egon. Her luxurious garment and carefully styled hair likely appealed to the novel's female readers.

4B.

24-552   25-576

4C.

In Illustration [21–480], Gretchen fends off the proposals of her suitor
Harald. He does not realize that his father is on Gretchen's revenge list
for a crime committed against her family. She travels to America where
Frau Trupp, a Pomeranian emigrant, cooks a fine German dinner of pick-
led pork, dumplings, and kraut. (WRK, p.471) This type of scene reinforced an image of national pride. After thirty years in America, Frau
Trupp still faithfully adheres to her German recipes.

In Illustration [92–2184], Leroy turns around and wonders who the
elderly gentleman intruding on him and Diana is. It is her father, accompanied by policemen. He tells Leroy that he has come to return his men-
tally deranged daughter to an institution. Leroy is shocked in disbelief.
Diana's face expresses sorrow and sadness for she has hidden the terrible truth from her suitor. She knows that her dream of escape and marriage to Leroy is shattered. She screams and says things which make no
sense. The father explains that the female side of the family is afflicted
with mental illness. The story within a story confirms the turn-of-the-
century conviction that insanity was mainly a female problem.

4C.

21-480

92-2184

5A. Luxury and Fancy Dresses

Illustration [52–1224] shows the Marquise Elena in the rich dress of a noblewoman. Her elbow is propped on a balustrade as she looks down at the beach and a boy who is bringing her a message.

Moonlight sparkles on the Mediterranean waves. The setting of Monte Carlo and Elena's demeanor give the reader a chance to experience vicariously the world of the rich. Mediterranean journeys were a privilege of the wealthy but, in the imagination, colportage readers could go there too. As so often in colportage, wealth comes with a burden: Elena is the target of a gang of criminal kidnappers.

5A. Luxury and Fancy Dresses

52-1224   76-1800

Edith's wealth, like Elena's, is manifested in her elaborately decorated and finely styled gown. In Illustration [76–1800], she is looking forward to an evening at the opera, unaware that a Parisian gang is planning to abduct her. Colportage readers were awed by novel characters' wealth and luxury, but, at the same time, this affluence attracted criminals who could bring misery to the "lucky" rich.

5B.

Illustration [97–2304] portrays Karla listening to the police chief of Vienna. He plans to arrest and prosecute the notorious dandy Egon. She, instead, wants to get Egon to force Bertha to leave Vienna so that Siegfried will turn his attention to Karla. She has become a wealthy lady. Her dress is trimmed with long fox furs.

In Illustration [81–1920] Countess Flora Urusow is taken aback by Siegfried's sudden appearance. Her lover, the Russian wrestler Kanzurow, has concocted a plan to use chloroform to make his rival Siegfried lose consciousness. Then he plans to throw Siegfried into a cage full of bears. Flora is the bait to lure Siegfried into the diabolical trap. The plumed hat, ruffled collar and matching umbrella, the flowing gown exude the distinction and luxury of nobility. Flora's duplicity and servility prove that even a noblewoman can be victim of an infatuation that normally only afflicts women of the lower classes in popular literature. (WRK, p.1918)

5B.

97-2304   81-1920

6A. Exotic Settings

Exotic foreign settings appealed to a reading public that heard about far-away places but could not afford to travel or experience such places personally. Illustration [39–912] shows Siegfried witnessing the Roman carnival parade led by carnival queen Violetta. Siegfried is about to toss a rose in Violetta's lap. Italy held a central place in the Germany imaginary, especially as an idealized setting for passion and romance, but also as a place of crime and old-fashioned banditry.

In Illustration [62–1464] the reader sees Siegfried observing the arrival of Prince Raisuli's corpse. His father, the sheik, acknowledges that Siegfried had killed his son in a fair battle and therefore bears no rancor against him. The exotic setting is spiced up by semi-nude women who bewail the young warrior's death. Siegfried's stint in the French Foreign Legion serves as an exciting episode in WRK. It would become the central theme to Büttner's 1914 novel Wanda, die Geliebte des Fremdenlegionärs. The novel was removed from the market by military, wartime censorship and ordered to be pulped in 1916.

6A. Exotic Settings

39-912   62-1464

6B.

The caption of Illustration [63–1488] refers to a Moroccan caravansary that is part of the Foreign Legion episode, yet the scene depicted shows a sort of Buffalo Bill figure and a stereotyped Indian smoking a pipe. How did the wrong exotic scene get placed in this section? Did a printer mistakenly insert an illustration for another novel instead of the correct one? Did the illustrator fail to deliver in time and the publisher had to come up with a makeshift replacement, hoping the customers would not notice? We will never have the answer but such sloppy work indicates something about how weekly or bi-weekly pamphlet publishing could be challenging.

A touch of oriental exoticism is included in the narrative about the San Francisco earthquake. Siegfried and Leroy tour Chinatown and visit a magic act where Siegfried volunteers to participate. In Illustration [34–793] Doly [sic], one of Siegfried's many female admirers, approaches the custodians of a funereal shipload of Chinese caskets sent from California back to the homeland. Siegfried is trapped in one of them. He did not realize that the Chinese magician had been bribed to imprison and kidnap him.

6B.

63-1488   34-793

6C.

Heinrich Büttner, the author of WRK, felt comfortable writing about the Middle East. In Illustration [64–1512] the Moroccan sultan offers Siegfried a taste of sybaritic orientalism. A dancing odalisque performs exclusively for the German guest. A mood of oriental eroticism is created in [W11-240], printed in Büttner's follow-up colportage novel <u>Wanda, die Geliebte des Fremdenlegionärs</u> (1914).

6C.

64-1512   W11-240

7A. The Mob and Violence

Viennese police keep an angry crowd at bay in Illustration [91–2160]. Rumor says a young woman has murdered her boyfriend. Individual members of the crowd have monstrous features and glare at the shocked, innocent young woman. Colportage novels showed the populace as volatile and always ready to apply "lynch justice."

In Illustration [71–1680], the helmsman stirs up a mutiny on a whaling ship as Karla and Siegfried look on. Here, too, the countenances, postures, and weapons, indicate the violent potential of crowds. The artist did not get the story straight because it is Egon who leads the mutiny, not the depicted helmsman. (WRK, p.1683) Like Siegfried and Karla, he remains loyal to the captain.

7B.

Russia, as a land of extremes, was a particularly attractive setting for melodrama and colportage writers. Beautiful Livia is a nihilist revolutionary who ends up in a tsarist jail in Illustration [83–1968]. Her supplications recall church imagery of martyred female saints. Illustration [85–2016] poignantly pictures the hanging of Livia. Her youthful innocence and idealism stands sharply against the vindictive rage of the crowd that relishes her execution. The moon and a flock of nocturnal birds add an eerie, Gothic aspect to the girl's cruel death. The melodramatic illustration marks a high point of the novel's artwork.

7B.

83-1968   85-2016

7C.

American settings were common in Wilhelmine colportage. Particularly the "Wild West" lent itself to harsh contrasts and tantalizing scenes of violence. Karl May's western colportage novels were bestsellers. Two of the most violent scenes in WRK take place in America. In Illustration [29–672] an immaculate Hilde stares in shock at the decapitated head of her American Indian suitor, Eagle Feather. Her carefully bound, flowing blonde hair bespeaks youthful innocence and German purity. She cannot fathom the meaning of the tousled, bloody hair and feathers attached to the lifeless head of the wild savage. In a modified manner, the melodramatic scene evokes the legend of Judith and Holofernes, an image oft-displayed in turn-of-the-century art.[3]

In Illustration [32–744], two horsemen prepare to rip the body of a captured bandit in half. A gleeful mob participates in this edition of an American lynching. Although disapproved by Siegfried, Leroy defends it as an expression of true and immediate popular justice.

7C.

29-672   32-744

8. Official Justice

The contrast between official and popular justice is a recurring theme of colportage literature and is manifested in WRK. In Illustration [5–96], Siegfried is wrongly accused of murder by a French court. The population correctly feels he is innocent and explodes in anger when the dusty and dry officials find him guilty. Clad in their robes and wearing judicial hats, the members of the court wait to watch Siegfried's beheading. In Illustration [7–144], a monstrous executioner rolls up his sleeves while Siegfried patiently awaits the guillotine's blade. The appearance of an executioner became *de rigueur* in colportage novels after the great success of Der Scharfrichrer von Berlin (The Executioner of Berlin, 1890) by Victor von Falk (pseudonym for Heinrich Sochaczewsky).

8. Official Justice

5-96

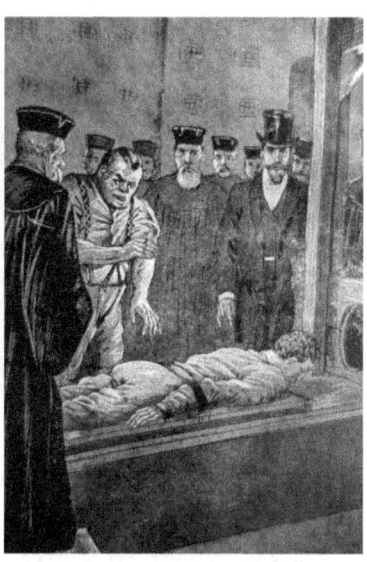

7-144

9.   Crime and Society

The criminal milieu was of great reader interest ever since Eugène Sue's
The Mysteries of Paris (1842–43). In Illustration [53–1248] the Italian thief
Filippo jumps from a window as he tries to escape. Illustration [69–1632],
an exceptionally well-drawn picture, shows a trio of criminals making
plans in a Hamburg pub. The two men listen attentively to the woman as
they await Egon, the initiator of practically all crime in WRK. On the wall
is a poster showing women dancing the cancan. To the left, at the next
table, Siegfried and Leroy try to eavesdrop on the three criminals.

9. Crime and Society

53-1248   69-1632

10. Trunks and Boxes

Being locked up in a trunk or suitcase, or being sealed up in a wall, or
"buried alive" – these are all standard ingredients of colportage. It hardly
requires a Freudian interpretation to recognize that there is an element
of repression and libidinal fantasy in these narratives of imprisonment
and release. In Illustration [4–72], Siegfried has been locked up in a trunk
by his rival Kara Achmed. The old trunk is bought by antiquarian collector
Lord Douglas. His daughter is curious to see what is inside and tries to
open it with several different keys. She can hardly believe her eyes when
she frees Siegfried from his dangerous confinement: "Now she thought
of nothing else but that he stood before her, he whose image had filled her
chaste dreams night after night. He, the youthful hero, whom she longed
for merely on account of his good looks, of his [media] image – he who
had taken her heart by storm." (WRK, p.97) Such an impossible story nevertheless appealed to colportage readers. They too could imagine their
very own Prince Charming emerge thankfully from a locked trunk. One
only had to find the key and all one's dreams became true. This imaginary
mechanism was a powerful colportage attraction for its subscribers. At
the same time, it was an object of ridicule and contempt for colportage's
many educated enemies.

Siegfried, in turn, releases Hilde from a nailed wooden box stored
with luggage on an American railway. In Illustration [26–600] a wall of
repression is broken down by the accidental discovery. Hilde embraces
her savior: "Your Hilde, my dear Siegfried. Your sister. Your lover. Your
bride!" (WRK, p.611) It may have been this titillating, transgressive subject of foster sibling love that eventually caused the removal of Hilde from
the story.

In Illustration [33–768] a Chinese magician had managed to lock
Siegfried into a trunk according to Egon's wishes. A confused Siegfried
steps out, asking where the magic show's audience and where his friend
Leroy are. Doly [sic] tells him, "You are in the land of miracles, stranger...
Come into my arms!" (WRK, p.779) Siegfried deliriously succumbs to
the charms of this young woman who was part of the Chinese magic act.
First, Doly is part of Egon's plot to kill Siegfried, but she later decides to
save him instead.

Trunks and Boxes

4-72   26-600   33-768

11.   Antisemitism

Jewish figures play a minor role in WRK. When they do appear, their depiction is not viciously antisemitic but works within a given cultural paradigm of prejudiced caricatures and clichès that are unflattering and vulgar. This is accentuated in the illustration [79–1872] of a very minor character who seeks to convince a Russian border official to approve his travel request. The portrayal includes the standard crooked nose, thick eyebrows, oversized ears, spindly hands, and large, floppy feet. The man's disposition is at once groveling and cunning. He is rebuffed until he offers a bribe of one hundred roubles. The marginal scene serves to expose Russian corruption and, by way of obvious omission, reinforces the reader's trust in the supposedly incorruptible German bureaucracy. Did colportage writers believe what they wrote or was this simply a manner of ingratiating themselves to a government pressured by zealous Schundkämpfer? Maybe they thought such indirect flattery of German officialdom would provide them with dividends when needed.

In Büttner's earlier novel Ferdinand Lassalle (1892–1893), the death of the hated Jewish moneylender Nathan Lewysohn (a fictitious character loaded with antisemitic stereotypes) is graphically illustrated adjacent to page 1824. A large stream of blood flows from the victim's neck down to the bedside carpet. This unusually bloody picture seems like a vengeful turnabout of the popular antisemitic image of "the Jew" as "bloodsucker." Reversing roles, here "the Jew" is the victim and the one who loses blood. (Lewysohn is called Blutsauger in Ferdinand Lassalle on page 310).

Antisemitism

79-1872   Ferdinand Lassalle - 1824

12. Incongruous Illustrations

Occasionally, incongruous illustrations show how swiftly pamphlet literature was produced and how prone it was to mistakes. We have already discussed the erroneous utilization of Illustration [63–1488]. In Illustration [71–1680] the picture misrepresents the story as the wrong character is shown leading a mutiny. Illustrations [72–1704] and [73–1728] reveal further novel weaknesses and lack of coordination between story writer and story illustrator. In the first scene, Karla encourages her unconscious, shipwrecked companion Siegfried to wake up. They are both dressed in sailor uniforms and have barely managed to save themselves by reaching a deserted island. The next illustration shows them weeks later, shortly before their rescue by a passing ship. Here Siegfried wears a comfortable, summer suit while Karla is dressed in a long gown. She also has flowing, blonde hair instead of dark, short curls and does not look at all like Karla the shipwrecked sailor in the previous picture. What went wrong between pamphlets 72 and 73?

Either a temporary substitute illustrator was not fully informed as to the section's content and thus could not provide a picture that fit the situation or made sense, or a picture from another novel was clumsily spliced into the required space (with the hope that subscribers and readers would not notice the discrepancies). It is also worth noting that in Wanda, die Geliebte des Fremdenlegionärs about a dozen illustrations from WRK are recycled. The only change is the caption under the picture which has been modified to fit the new publication. The Dresdner Roman-Verlag bought the illustrations from the Weichert Verlag and distributed them here and there in their new Büttner novel. Surely, loyal Büttner readers would have been unhappy with this cheap trick

Incongruous Illustrations

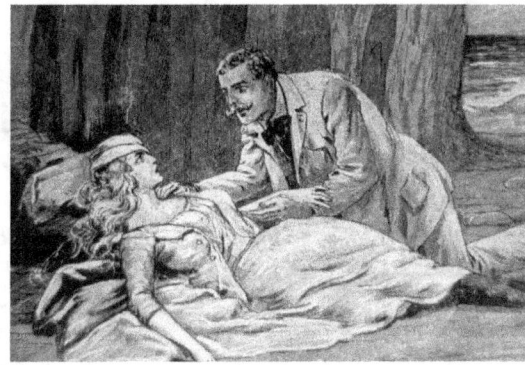

73-1728

72-1704

13. Serial Novel Wrapper Covers

Illustrated here are pamphlet covers from Büttner's novels <u>Das Weib des Ringkämpfers</u> (1906–1907) and <u>Wanda, die Geliebte des Fremdenlegionärs</u> (1914). The <u>WRK</u> cover shows Siegfried in his wrestler's outfit with bell bars behind him as well as wreathes and bows given to the world champion wrestler. Siegfried, muscular arms folded, looks off into the distance. He seems aloof and disinterested in the woman supplicating attention at his feet. This is not the Siegfried of the novel, who shows great interest in every woman he meets, always exclaiming, "She is the most beautiful woman I have ever seen."

Nor is the woman with long, flowing black hair his wife Bertha. She is described on page 1314 as having blonde, curly hair. Why is the cover not compatible with the story? The problem in designing a colportage novel is that the novel was a work in progress in its initial stages. If the author only had a hazy idea as to the shape and contents of the novel, how could the illustrator design a suitable cover? For this reason, the covers of Büttner's 1907 and 1914 novels have an identical sort of melodramatic format intended to capture customer interest in a general way.

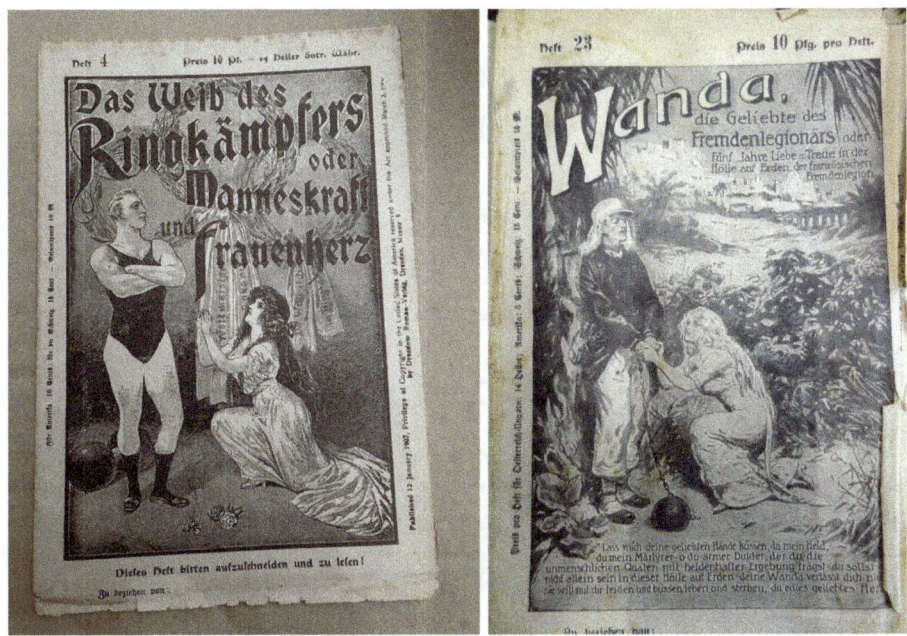

Left: Das Weib des Ringkämpfers, 1907 (Courtesy of Wolfgang Kaiser).
Right: Wanda, die Geliebte des Fremdenlegionärs, (1914) (Courtesy of DLA, Marbach).

Notes

Three Readers: George Grosz, Moritz Bromme, Adelheid Popp

1   George Grosz, Ein kleines Ja und ein grosses Nein (Hamburg: Rowohlt, 1955), 23.
2   Ibid.
3   Some of these titles I could not find in the Kosch catalogue. Some were slightly different from those in the bibliography. Günter Kosch and Manfrd Nagl, Der Kolportage Roman (Stuttgart: J.B.Metzler Verlag, 1993).
4   Grosz, 24.
5   Ibid.
6   See my Weimar Controversies: Explorations in Popular Culture with Siegfried Kracauer (Bielefeld: transcript, 2020), 70.
7   Grosz, 24.
8   Moritz Bromme, Lebensgeschichte eines modernen Fabrikarbeiters (Frankfurt: Athenäum, 1971 reprint of 1905 edition), 77–78.
9   Ibid., 78.
10 Ibid., 116.
11 Ibid., 117.
12 Adelheid Popp, Die Jugendgeschichte einer Arbeiterin (Berlin: Dietz, 1922), 13.
13 Ibid., 14.
14 Martina Tichy, Alltag und Traum (Wien: Hermann Böhlaus Nachf., 1984), 88.
15 Ibid., 85.

16   Ibid., 86.
17   Popp, 43–44.
18   Ibid. 43–44.

For and Against Popular Literature

1   Janice Radway, Reading the Romance: Women, Patriarchy, and Popular Literature (Chapel Hill: University of North Carolina, Press, 1984), 100.
2   Ibid., 89.
3   Ibid., 85.
4   Lynn Abrams, Workers' Culture in Imperial Germany (London: Routledge, 1992), 105.
5   Ibid., 155.
6   Ibid., 150.
7   Ibid., 173.
8   Ibid., 109.
9   Friedrich Rommel, Pädagogisches Archiv. Jg.53 (1911) Heft 2.,74.
10   Ibid., 74.
11   Ibid.
12   Ibid., 75.
13   Ibid.
14   Ibid., 74.
15   Pretorius, "Der Kolportageroman: Eine Literar-historische Studie," Die neue Welt, vol.22 (1897), 34.
16   Lilli Janosch, "Glossen zur Ausstellung gegen die Schundlitertatur," Ethische Kultur, vol.19 (1911), 28.
17   Ernst Schultze, Die Schundliteratur (Halle: Verlag der Buchhändler des Waisenhauses, 1911), 150.
18   Ibid., 11.
19   Ibid., 15.
20   Ibid., 37.
21   Ibid., 71.

22   See Dietrich Kerlen, "Protestantismus und Buchverehrung in Deutschland," Jahrbuch für Kommunikationsgeschichte, 1 Jg. (1999). 1–22.

23   Schultze, 15.

24   Ibid., 51.

25   Ibid., 62.

26   Ibid., 51.

27   Ibid., 91.

28   Ibid., 147.

29   Ibid., 151.

30   Ibid., 40.

31   Günter Kosch und Manfred Nagl, Der Kolportage Roman (Stuttgart: Metzler, 1993).

Enter Siegfried the Wrestler

1   Heinrich Büttner, Das Weib des Ringkämpfers oder Manneskraft und Frauenherz (Dresden: Dresdner Roman-Verlag, 1907), 12.

2   WRK., 16.

3   Ibid., 17.

4   Ibid., 20.

5   Ibid., 24.

6   Ibid.

7   See Philip Ajouri, "Der Cliffhanger im Kolportageroman um 1900," KulturPoetik Band 21, Heft 1 (2021), 47–69.

Wrestling

1   Benjamin Litherland, Wrestling in Britain (London: Routledge, 2018) Litherland quotes Charles B. Cochran from Secrets of a Showman. 60.

2   WRK., 898.

3   Ibid., 568.

4   Ibid., 571.
5   Vorwärts, "Sport und Geschäft," 26.2.1905.
6   WRK., 1559.
7   Ibid., 1897.
8   Ibid., 1902.
9   Ibid., 1909.
10   Ibid., 2127.

National and Ethnic Stereotypes

1   Mark Hewitson, Germany and the Modern World 1880–1914 (Cambridge: Cambridge University Press, 2018), 225.
2   WRK., 1383.
3   Ibid., 1913.
4   Ibid., 2196.
5   Ibid., 2211.
6   Ibid.
7   Ibid., 1433.
8   Ibid., 1444.
9   Ibid., 1470.
10   Ibid., 1468.
11   Ibid., 756–757.
12   Ibid., 758.
13   Ibid., 635.
14   Ibid., 645.
15   Ibid., 655.
16   Ibid., 954.
17   Ibid., 360.
18   Ibid., 659.
19   Ibid., 898.
20   Ibid., 400.
21   Ibid., 431.
22   Ibid., 478.
23   Ibid., 420.

24 Ibid., 748.
25 Deutscher Herold, (Sioux Falls, South Dakota), Dec.28, 1916.
26 Deutscher Herold, March 19, 1914.
27 WRK, 202.
28 Ibid., 145.
29 Ibid., 1044.
30 Ibid., 1910.
31 Ibid., 1903
32 Ibid., 1913.
33 Ibid., 1949.
34 Ibid., 1950.
35 Ibid., 1952.
36 Ibid., 1962.
37 Ibid., 1991.
38 Ibid., 1984.
39 Ibid., 1986.

Current Events and Sensation

1   WRK, 2066.
2   Ibid., 2073.
3   Ibid.. 2080.
4   Ibid., 2084.
5   Ibid., 2105.
6   Ibid., 2107.
7   Ibid., 2123.
8   Vorwärts, September 1, 1903.
9   Vorwärts,, July 23, 1903.
10 Ibid.
11 Vossische Zeitung, April 20, 1906. No.183, Abendausgabe.
12 WRK, 752.
13 Ibid., 755.
14 Ibid., 806–807.
15 Ibid., 807.

16   Ibid., 811.
17   Elaine Hadley, Melodramatic Tactics (Stanford: Stanford University Press, 1995), 68.
18   Ibid., 112.

Class Conflict: Siegfried as Peacemaker

1   WRK, 1384.
2   Ibid., 1336.
3   Ibid., 1339.
4   Ibid., 1302.
5   Ibid., 1308.
6   Ibid., 1310.
7   Ibid., 1311.
8   Ibid., 1400.
9   Ibid., 1403.
10   Ibid., 1407.

Wilhelmine Women and their Wrestler

1   WRK, 258.
2   Ibid., 262.
3   Ibid.
4   Ibid., 268.
5   Ibid., 269.
6   Ibid., 275.
7   Ibid.
8   Ibid., 283.
9   Ibid., 406.
10   Ibid., 927.
11   Ibid., 941.
12   Ibid., 1112.
13   Ibid., 1104.

14   Ibid., 2126.

15   Ibid., 2135.

16   Ibid., 2393.

17   Ibid., 2395.

18   Thomas Batty (1832–1903) was an English lion tamer and circus owner.

19   WRK., 578.

20   Ibid., 921.

21   Ibid., 2190.

The Contradictions of Colportage: Paternalism and Populism

1   WRK, 2198.

2   Ibid., 1918.

3   Ibid., 1290.

4   Ibid., 747–8.

5   Ibid, 1132.

6   Ibid., 1139.

7   Ibid., 1137.

8   On this subject, see Esther Sabelus„ Die weisse Sklavin (Berlin: Panama Verlag, 2009).

9   WRK, 1368.

10   Ibid., 748.

11   Ibid., 1433.

12   Ibid., 1067.

13   Ibid., 1851.

14   Ibid., 1872.

15   Ibid., 2395.

16   Ibid., 2396.

Postscript: Heinrich Büttner's First Colportage Novel of 1892

1   Heinrich Büttner, Ferdinand Lassalle (Berlin: Friedrichs und Co., 1892–93), 308.
2   Ibid., 311.
3   Ibid., 543–544.
4   Ibid., 1172.
5   Vorwärts, February 2, 1892.
6   Ibid., February 10, 1892.

The Illustrations

1   Jessica Ellen Plummer, Selling Fiction: the German Colportage Novel 1871–1914 (University of Texas Ph.D, Austin, 2016).
2   For the theme of powerful, evil women see Bram Dijsktra, Idols of Perversity: Fantasies of Feminine Evil in Fin-de-Siecle Culture (New York: Oxford University Press, 1986).
3   To this interest, see also Dijkstra.

Historical Sciences

Aurora G. Morcillo
**(In)visible Acts of Resistance
in the Twilight of the Franco Regime**
A Historical Narration

January 2022, 332 p., pb., ill.
50,00 € (DE), 978-3-8376-5257-4
E-Book: available as free open access publication
PDF: ISBN 978-3-8394-5257-8

Jesús Muñoz Morcillo, Caroline Y. Robertson-von Trotha (eds.)
Genealogy of Popular Science
From Ancient Ecphrasis to Virtual Reality

2020, 586 p., pb., col. ill.
49,00 € (DE), 978-3-8376-4835-5
E-Book:
PDF: 48,99 € (DE), ISBN 978-3-8394-4835-9

Monika Ankele, Benoît Majerus (eds.)
Material Cultures of Psychiatry

2020, 416 p., pb., col. ill.
40,00 € (DE), 978-3-8376-4788-4
E-Book: available as free open access publication
PDF: ISBN 978-3-8394-4788-8

**All print, e-book and open access versions of the titles in our list
are available in our online shop www.transcript-publishing.com!**

Historical Sciences

Ulrike Brunotte
The Femininity Puzzle
Gender, Orientalism and the »Jewish Other«

September 2022, 236 p., pb., col. ill.
45,00 € (DE), 978-3-8376-5821-7
E-Book:
PDF: 44,99 € (DE), ISBN 978-3-8394-5821-1

Andreas Kraß, Moshe Sluhovsky, Yuval Yonay (eds.)
Queer Jewish Lives Between Central Europe and Mandatory Palestine
Biographies and Geographies

January 2022, 332 p., pb., ill.
39,99 € (DE), 978-3-8376-5332-8
E-Book:
PDF: 39,99 € (DE), ISBN 978-3-8394-5332-2

Sascha R. Klement
Representations of Global Civility
English Travellers in the Ottoman Empire
and the South Pacific, 1636–1863

2021, 270 p., pb.
45,00 € (DE), 978-3-8376-5583-4
E-Book:
PDF: 44,99 € (DE), ISBN 978-3-8394-5583-8

**All print, e-book and open access versions of the titles in our list
are available in our online shop www.transcript-publishing.com!**

GPSR Authorized Representative: Easy Access System Europe, Mustamäe tee
50, 10621 Tallinn, Estonia, gpsr.requests@easproject.com